SIMP
SONI
STAS
VOL. 4

Tales from *New Literary Project*

SIMP SONI STAS

VOL. 4

EDITED BY JOSEPH DI PRISCO

RARE BIRD
LOS ANGELES, CALIF.

RARE BIRD

THIS IS A GENUINE RARE BIRD BOOK

Rare Bird Books
6044 North Figueroa Street
Los Angeles, CA 90042
rarebirdbooks.com

FIRST TRADE PAPERBACK ORIGINAL EDITION

For more information, address:
Rare Bird Books Subsidiary Rights Department
6044 North Figueroa Street
Los Angeles, CA 90042

This is a work of fiction and a product of the author's imagination.
Names, characters, businesses, places, events, and incidents are used in a
fictitious manner. Any resemblance to actual persons, living or dead,
or actual events is purely coincidental

Set in Minion
Printed in the United States

Proceeds from book sales go toward supporting the work of
the nonprofit New Literary Project, newliteraryproject.org

10 9 8 7 6 5 4 3 2 1

Library of Congress Cataloging-in-Publication Data available upon request

Sept 2025

For Peter —

Onward!

Dedicated to
Simpson Workshops writers
And younger writers everywhere

In friendship,

CONTENTS

NOTES & ACKNOWLEDGMENTS

Grateful thanks to authors and publishers for generous permission to print or reprint.

"Alcatraz" from THE OFFICE OF HISTORICAL CORRECTIONS: A NOVELLA AND STORIES by Danielle Evans, copyright © 2020 by Danielle Evans. Used by permission of Riverhead, an imprint of Penguin Publishing Group, a division of Penguin Random House LLC. All rights reserved.

"At the Round Earth's Imagined Corners" from FLORIDA by Lauren Groff, copyright © 2018 by Lauren Groff. Used by permission of Riverhead, an imprint of Penguin Publishing Group, a division of Penguin Random House LLC. All rights reserved.

"Entering Uncertainty: Revelations of the Blank Page," by Lorne Buchman. Excerpted from *Make to Know: From Spaces of Uncertainty to Creative Discovery*, by Lorne M. Buchman *Make to Know: From Spaces of Uncertainty to Creative Discovery* © 2021 Thames & Hudson Ltd Text © 2021 Lorne M. Buchman. Reprinted by permission of Thames & Hudson Inc, www.thamesandhudsonusa.com

"The Happy Place," by Joyce Carol Oates, copyright 2021 by Ontario Review, Inc.; published in *The (Other) You* (Ecco, an imprint of HarperCollins Publishers). Reprinted with permission of the author.

"Jenna Takes the Fall," by A. R. Taylor, originally published in, and excerpted from, *Jenna Takes the Fall* (She Writes Press), reprinted with permission of the publisher and the author.

"On Saying Goodbye to Possibly My Favorite Place on Earth," by Anthony Marra, originally published on *Lithub*, reprinted with permission of the author.

"Passenger X," by John Murray, originally published in *Origins Journal*, reprinted with permission of the author.

Poems by Jessica Laser, originally published in *Sergei Kuzmich from All Sides* (Letter Machine Editions, 2019). Reprinted with permission of the author.

Poems by Ralph J. Long Jr., originally published in *Polaroids at a Yard Sale* (Main Street Rag Publishing Company, 2021). Reprinted with permission of the author.

"STRONG TIES and Strong-Ties," by Katharine Ogden Michaels, originally published *Strong Ties: Barclay Simpson and the Pursuit of the Common Good in Business and Philanthropy*, Katharine Ogden Michaels with Judith K. Adamson (Rare Bird Books); copyright by Katharine Ogden Michaels; reprinted with permission of the publisher and the author.

Simpsonistas: Tales from the Simpson Literary Project Vol. 1 (2018)

Simpsonistas: Tales from the Simpson Literary Project Vol. 2 (2019)

Simpsonistas: Tales from the Simpson Literary Project Vol. 3 (2021)

Simpsonistas: Tales from New Literary Project Vol. 4 (2022)

Series Editor: Joseph Di Prisco

PEOPLE, PLACES, & THINGS
A MISCELLANY

The University of California, Berkeley, English Department. english.berkeley.edu/

Department Chairs, 2016–2022:
Prof. Genaro Padilla, Prof. Steven Justice, Prof. Ian Duncan, Prof. Eric Falci
The University of California, Berkeley. berkeley.edu/

Simpson Project Writing Workshops, Spring 2022—

Cal Prep. The Richmond Aspire California College Preparatory Academy is a public charter and early college secondary school, cofounded by University of California, Berkeley, and Aspire Public Schools. Tatiana Lim-Breitbart, Principal.

Contra Costa County Juvenile Hall, Martinez, California; Mt. McKinley High School, Contra Costa County Office of Education. Robert Bowers, Principal.

Girls Inc. of Alameda County; Julayne Virgil, CEO; Gabi Reyes-Acosta, Jazmin Noble, Aja Holland, Carina Silva. girlsinc-alameda.org/

Northgate High School, Mount Diablo Unified School District; David Wood, faculty; northgatehighschool.org/

Simpson Fellows: Workshop Leaders 2017–2022
University of California, Berkeley, English Department—

Prof. Fiona McFarlane, Director

Uttara Chaudhuri

Frank Cruz

Katherine Ding

Delarys Ramos Estrada

Lise Gaston

John James

Ryan Lackey

Jessica Laser

Ismail Muhammad

Laura Ritland

Alex Ullman

Rosetta Young

Noah Warren

Jack Hazard Fellows: Summer 2022
Creative Writers Teaching High School
Open to applicants from high schools throughout the nation for Summer 2023—

Prof. Ian S. Maloney, Director

Kevin Allardice (Albany High School)

Julie T. Anderson (The College Preparatory School)

Armando Batista (Pacific Ridge School)

Adam O. Davis (The Bishop's School)

Sheila Madary (Saint Mary's High School)

Molly Montgomery (Emery High School)

Mehnaz Sahibzada (New Roads School)

Andy Spear (Head-Royce School)

Tori Sciacca (Richmond High School)

Joyce Carol Oates Prize
2017–2022

Awarded annually, $50,000, not for a book, but to a distinguished
mid-career author of fiction, that is, one who has emerged and is still emerging.

2022 Joyce Carol Oates Prize Finalists

Christopher Beha

Percival Everett

Lauren Groff (Prize Recipient)

Katie Kitamura

Jason Mott

2021 Joyce Carol Oates Prize Finalists

Danielle Evans (Prize Recipient)

Jenny Offill

Darin Strauss

Lysley Tenorio

2020 Joyce Carol Oates Prize Finalists

    Chris Bachelder

    Maria Dahvana Headley

    Rebecca Makkai

    Daniel Mason (Prize Recipient)

    Peter Orner

    Dexter Palmer

    Kevin Wilson

2019 Joyce Carol Oates Prize Finalists

    Rachel Kushner

    Laila Lalami (Prize Recipient)

    Valeria Luiselli

    Sigrid Nunez

    Anne Raeff

    Amor Towles

2018 Joyce Carol Oates Prize Finalists

    Ben Fountain

    Samantha Hunt

    Karan Mahajan

    Anthony Marra (Prize Recipient)

    Martin Pousson

2017 Joyce Carol Oates Prize Finalists

    T. Geronimo Johnson (Prize Recipient)

    Valeria Luiselli

    Lori Ostlund

    Dana Spiotta

Joyce Carol Prize Longlisted Authors' Publishers: 2017–2022
(with number of their authors listed)

    Algonquin (7)

    Back Bay (1)

    Bellevue Literary (3)

Bloomsbury (5)

Catapult (3)

Celadon (1)

Coffee House (1)

Counterpoint (11)

Custom House (1)

Delphinium (1)

Dial (2)

Doubleday (4)

Dutton (2)

Dzanc (1)

Ecco (17)

Elixir (1)

Flatiron (1)

FSG (13)

Grand Central (1)

Graywolf (7)

Grove (4)

Harper Collins/William Morrow (3) (2017 Prize Recipient)

Henry Holt (1)

Hogarth (3) (2018 Prize Recipient)

Houghton Mifflin (4)

Knopf (11)

Little, Brown (14) (2020 Prize Recipient)

Mariner (1)

MCD/FSG (7)

Melville House (1)

Nan A. Talese (1)

New York Review of Books (1)

Norton (7)

Pantheon (2) (2019 Prize Recipient)

Penguin (13)

Picador (2)

Putnam (6)

Random House (6)

Rare Bird (2)

Riverhead (24) (2021 and 2022 Prize Recipients)

Simon & Schuster (5)

Soft Skull (1)

Soho (4)

St Martin's (4)

Tim Duggan (1)

Tin House (2)

Viking (6)

238 Longlisted Authors

47 Publishers

31 Finalists

6 Prize Recipients (drawn from 5 publishers)

Jurors (in rotation) for the Joyce Carol Oates Prize 2017-2022:

Heidi Benson

Anne Cain

Joseph Di Prisco

Professor Joshua Gang

Jane Hu

Professor Donna Jones

Regan McMahon

Professor Geoffrey O'Brien

Professor Katherine Snyder

David Wood

Professor Dora Zhang

Deep gratitude to the awesome Vickie Sciacca for kindly, masterful coordination.

FOREWORD

DIANE DEL SIGNORE
EXECUTIVE DIRECTOR

Simpsonistas: Tales from New Literary Project: Vol. 4 celebrates the range of interests and the diverse work associated with the various artists, young and old, emerged and still emerging, accomplished as well as fledgling— all of them writers who speak in their individual voices to our collective purpose. In other words, our writers bravely write their hearts out, across generations, communities, and divides. All of them, in their distinct ways, drive social change by lifting up a literate, democratic society.

Herein you will discover extraordinary writing from four Joyce Carol Oates Prize Recipients—Danielle Evans, Lauren Groff, Daniel Mason, and Anthony Marra—together with Joyce Carol Oates herself. Right alongside these worthies, you will read moving and promising work from some of the younger writers in our Simpson Workshops and from three of their workshop leaders of the Berkeley English Department, as well as a Simpson Fellow Alumna. In addition, we are fortunate to include stories, essays, and poems from graduates of the workshops as well as many other talented, devoted friends and colleagues and associates of New Literary Project. The only entry qualification is that the writer be a Simpsonista.

But what exactly is a Simpsonista?

Be advised: Once you cross paths with a Simpsonista, you may never be the same. For the truth is, a Simpsonista is an extraordinary creature, variously at home in the city or in the wild, from Brooklyn to LA, Chicago to Seattle, DC to Portland, Austin to Berkeley. Step lightly when approaching. They can be discovered in solitary contemplation or in teeming community, it all depends. A Simpsonista is a storyteller and a teacher, a novelist and/or a short story writer, a passionate defender of artistic freedom, a courageous encourager of leaps toward literature as well as literacy, an avid reader and a dedicated writer, a student and a professor, a librarian and a high school teacher, a publisher and an editor. You know what? If you love a great story, you yourself just may be a budding Simpsonista.

We hope you enjoy our new anthology. (If you're curious, earlier Volumes 1, 2, and 3 hold manifold delights and challenges in store as well.) And consult our website, please, to find out more about New Literary Project, which was founded in 2016. That is where you will find videos and color about all our initiatives: **Jack Hazard Summer Fellowships**, for creative writers who teach high school; **Simpson Writing Workshops**, offered at no cost to communities of younger writers at places like Girls Inc. of Alameda County, Contra Costa Juvenile Hall, and elsewhere; **Simpson Fellowships**, for creative writing teachers who are graduate students at Cal; the **Joyce Carol Oates Prize**, the annual major national award to a mid-career author of fiction; and the **Simpsonista Award**, for an inspiring someone who helps give voice to writers and storytellers across the generations.

One of those Simpsonista Award Winners, Julayne Virgil, CEO of Girls Inc. of Alameda County—where NewLit has conducted writing workshops every year of our existence—memorably said this: "These girls are very vulnerable. There's a question of: Who is allowed to tell stories? Whose stories matter? Am I really supposed to share this?" (*Datebook, San Francisco Chronicle*, 5/28/22; Anna Nordberg) "Giving girls the confidence that their voice, their story, their art matters"—and that "how they view the world is meaningful"—can be transformative, Julayne said. She remembers one New Literary Project showcase where a father wept listening to his daughter read her work. "This is so important for her," he told Julayne. "She'll never be the same."

Neither will any of us.

AN INTRODUCTION:
QUESTION & ANSWER

JOSEPH DI PRISCO

Q: As everyone knows—

A: Gonna stop you right there. What exactly does *everyone* know and who exactly is *everyone*?

Q: All right, if that's the way it's going to be. Is our country broken?

A: How much time you have?

Q: Hey, it's your dime. Is our country broken?

A: What do you think?

Q: Didn't anybody explain how the Q & A thing works? I ask the questions, you answer them.

A: I'm not always sure what works anymore. Think about it: Pandemic. Ukraine. Children massacred, sitting ducks in their classroom desks. Police violence. Systemic racism. Racial inequality. Transphobia. Homophobia. Coup conspiracy in plain view. AR-15 fetish. Daily mass shootings and murders. Autocrat fan boys in the bleachers. Pregnant women statutorily compelled to give birth. Bounty hunting on gynecologists. Year-round fire season and drought. Climate apocalypse.

Q. That's just about the worst Billy Joel song ever.

A: Who's Billy Joel?

Q: Let's try again. Is our country broken?

A: Whose country is *our* country? Because it's going gangbusters for the plutocrats and the minority/majority politicians who rule the roost.

Q: Not sure I am following you.

A: Go watch *The Wire* again. You think anything's changed?

Q: Old school TV allusion? Man, you gotta update your priors. But then: Steven Pinker's better angels. The world's more peaceable than it's been for ages. Scientific advances. The remediation of disease. Non-carbon energy sources. And so on and so on.

A: Tell the Russians. Tell the singing elephants being poached. Tell the kids doing active shooter drills in their schools. Tell the epidemiologists. You're asking questions you really don't want to hear the answer to.

Q: Depressing.

A: You're finally getting it, it's all very depressing.

Q: I mean you're depressing.

A: I rest your case.

Q: Let's get to the main topic, time's running out.

A: We have a topic? Brilliant. Go for it.

Q: Why bother to read, to write, to make art if things are as screwed up, as threatening, as unstable as you say? Seems trivial in the grand scheme of things.

A: In the grand scheme of things there may be no grand scheme of things.

Q: There you go, contradicting yourself again.

A: Or to quote Joyce Carol Oates, our guiding light: "My belief is that art should not be comforting; for comfort, we have mass entertainment and one another. Art should provoke, disturb, arouse our emotions, expand our sympathies in directions we may not anticipate and may not even wish."

Q: That doesn't respond to my question, but it makes more sense than you've offered so far.

A: You got a better idea what to do with our limited time on this endangered planet? I'll assume not. But here's what Toni Morrison wrote a long time ago, and it's nonetheless true even if people keep quoting that genius over and over again, because nobody ever said it better:

This is precisely the time when artists go to work. There is no time for despair, no place for self-pity, no need for silence, no room for fear. We speak, we write, we do language. That is how civilizations heal. I know the world is bruised and bleeding, and though it is important not to ignore its pain, it is also critical to refuse to succumb to its malevolence. Like failure, chaos contains information that can lead to knowledge—even wisdom. Like art.

Q: That's your drop-the-mic *better to light a candle than curse the darkness* moment?

A: That's my story, and I'm....

Q: Have you missed the last ten, twenty, thirty, fifty years of American politics? You harbor some pretty high-minded, downright impractical notions about art and artists, don't you?

A: Just the opposite. It's all every bit as practical and fundamental as food, as water, as the air we breathe and as urgent. Here's what James Baldwin said during a radio interview in 1962, and don't forget it:

> You survive this and in some terrible way, which I suppose no one can ever describe, you are compelled, you are corralled, you are bullwhipped into dealing with whatever it is that hurt you. And what is crucial here is that if it hurt you, that is not what's important. Everybody's hurt. What is important, what corrals you, what bullwhips you, what drives you, torments you, is that you must find some way of using this to connect you with everyone else alive. This is all you have to do it with. You must understand that your pain is trivial except insofar as you can use it to connect with other people's pain; and insofar as you can do that with your pain, you can be released from it, and then hopefully it works the other way around too; insofar as I can tell you what it is to suffer, perhaps I can help you to suffer less.... I really don't like words like "artist" or "integrity" or "courage" or "nobility." I have a kind of distrust of all those words because I don't really know what they mean, any more than I really know what such words as "democracy" or "peace" or "peace-loving"

or "warlike" or "integration" mean. And yet one is compelled to recognize that all these imprecise words are attempts made by us all to get to something which is real and which lives behind the words. Whether I like it or not, for example, and no matter what I call myself, I suppose the only word for me, when the chips are down, is that I am an artist. There is such a thing. There is such a thing as integrity. Some people are noble. There is such a thing as courage. The terrible thing is that the reality behind these words depends ultimately on what the human being (meaning every single one of us) believes to be real. The terrible thing is that the reality behind all these words depends on choices one has got to make, for ever and ever and ever, every day. (*The Cross of Redemption: Uncollected Writings*; Vintage International; Randal Kenan, ed.)

Q: .

A: That's the perfect question you have there. As for Baldwin: that's some kind of kickass anti-manifesto manifesto, isn't it? I reject—and NewLit rejects—the cynicism at the center of those interrogations into the futility of art in our rocked and troubled world. It's too self-serving, reeks too much of drama-queen syndrome. Boo hoo. Sure, at the same time, we will ask them of ourselves, we're human, we get discouraged, we lose faith. There's a raft of bad news out there, more rolling in by the day. But then we find it again and lose it again and find it again and again in unexpected places, during unanticipated moments, and if we're lucky, we get to keep it for a while, an hour, a day, another day, and days leak into weeks, and maybe we can shape an entire existence, a lifetime, not of unfettered dreamy hopefulness so much as steely resolve, as strength, as a few minutes of fearlessness, which is just long enough to write a poem, or even one sentence that leads to other sentences, and before you know it, a work of art appears, a story, a novel, a poem, if we are capable and if we want it badly enough, and that finally is on the verge of being enough. Because what does *finally* mean except *now*, when we need art, and, guess what, art needs us, too, in order to remind everyone once again that we are alive for a little while longer, that we have survived, finally—for now.

Q: You haven't convinced me.

A: But now that you're here, it is your choice, whether or not to read the NewLit writers gathered here. Some of them are very young, some not so much. All of them, like you in your darkest, loneliest hours, are grappling with the facts of their own mortality and the besiegement of our country, the ravishment of our world. Art, like life itself, is a story of taking the risk on making and embracing meaningfulness, in our case, the risk of making a choice for yourself to write and read your heart out. You know how people still say, "It is what it is"? As in, *Deal with it*, or *Grow up already*, maybe *Be Zen about it*. Part disconsolation, part acceptance? Like that? Yeah, well, I never said *It is what it is* once in my life. To me, *It is what it is* means being unfashionably late to the party, only it's the wrong party, where you weren't invited in the first place. Worse than that, whose idea was this shirt you're wearing? Or it's being early, and it's the right party but nobody else is going to show, they're at a different, better party, and you can't get an Uber in this part of town. And you realize, I think I hate parties. It never is what it is.

Q: On that note, I think our time is up. Thank you.

A: Wrong again, we're just getting started.

ALCATRAZ

DANIELLE EVANS
2021 JOYCE CAROL OATES PRIZE RECIPIENT

Everyone had told me that Alcatraz was nothing but a tourist trap, but I was desperate that summer for anything that would give my mother a sense of closure, and it seemed fortuitous that the prison that had opened all the wounds in the first place was right in the middle of the water I could see from the window of my new apartment. I hadn't come to the Bay on purpose—a string of coincidences and a life I hadn't known I'd wanted until I got there brought me to Oakland. Still, almost since the day I had arrived, it seemed like the only thing keeping me from the island was deliberate avoidance. I felt like I'd gotten it backward. Everyone else I'd met who'd come to California from the East Coast was running away from something, and I'd gone and gotten so close to the sting of the past that it sometimes seemed like I could touch it.

I had come west to work at an experimental after-school theater and dance therapy program for children who had been abused. A friend I'd gone to college with spent months recruiting me, sending me literature about the program: smiling children's faces, photographs of the Bay and the Pacific. I was sold on the adventure, on the postcard-perfect water's specific shade of blue, but by the time I said yes, she'd decided to move to Texas to begin a PhD program. I went anyway—I was twenty-four and convinced that the life in which I made some critically important difference to everyone around me could start on my command, that the world was only waiting to know what I asked of it. I was anxious and exhausted all the time then, but I remember those days now as being filled with optimism, a sense of possibility.

The organization's budget was so strained that our supervisors worked for free some months when we were between grants. I made ends meet tutoring and doing SAT prep for kids in Berkeley and Marin County. Two of our college student volunteers quit after working at the center for less than a week—one of them had her cell phone stolen and the other was cursed out by four different kids, in three different languages. My own first week on the job, a child had threatened to stab me with a pencil, but by and large I loved the work I did, the crayon drawings and earnest thank-you letters I got to pin to my wall, the way kids who used to greet me with skittishness at best, open contempt and hostility at worst, started running to hug me when I walked through the door.

My mother had never been to the West Coast and didn't like that I was there. We were East Coast people and this coast had done us wrong, almost kept us from existing. My great-grandfather had done time here—had been kept in the basement of Alcatraz, and been told every day that when he was dead they would feed him to the rats. He was eighteen then, finally of legal age to be in the army, except he'd been in it three years already thanks to a falsified birth certificate. It was 1920 and Alcatraz was still a military prison, infamous not for its gangsters but among would-be deserters. They were still building the parts of the prison that would later be immortalized, but it was already enough of a prison to be Charles Sullivan's private hell, the one he never really left, the one my mother, God bless her, was still trying to redeem.

My mother was born nearly four decades later, born at all because after two years, the army, with the help of his appointed lawyer, admitted their mistake. They cleared him of murder and told him he was free to go. He took the long way back to the Bronx—spent years trying to make himself homes in inhospitable places—but when he finally arrived back in New York, he married Louise, the first woman who took pity on him, and they had two children, the younger of whom was my grandmother. I never met her; she left a few months after my mother—a brown girl in a white family—was born. When my mother was six, a neighbor told her to her face that her own mother was too ashamed to stay in the house and claim her. After she came home crying, Charlie Sullivan pricked his finger and then hers and pressed them together and said they had the same blood now and whatever she was he was too, but my mother was too young to have heard of the one-drop rule and the intention was lost on her until years later. My mother called her grandparents Grammy and Papa: Grammy was firmly assigned the role of grandparent because they all chose to believe her mother might return someday, but Papa was her everything. When she was thirteen, her Grammy died, and my mother belatedly came to appreciate what she had done while alive—squirreled away money before Papa spent it, saw to it that the rent was paid and the heat was on and everyone in the house had clean clothes and three meals a day, and that her husband stayed sober enough to work, except when he had the prison nightmares, and had to be kept drunk enough not to wake the neighbors with screams.

At eighteen, my mother left home for college. She only went as far as Jersey, but her grandfather was dead within two years of her going. It wouldn't occur to me until well into my adulthood, most of it spent in California, a full country away from her, to question my mother's conviction that the former event had caused the latter, or to wonder what she wanted me to do with a cautionary tale in which the caution was against growing up.

By the time she came to visit me in Oakland, my mother had been involved in some form of litigation or negotiation with the US government for the better part of twenty years. Her latest calculations— which she had me double-check annually, adding the accrued interest— concluded that the US government owed us $227,035.87. She wanted the number exact so that we did not seem unreasonable. I was a kid when she started the complaint process, first with letters to the Board for Correction of Military records, the same board her grandfather had been writing letters to for years before he died. This was right after my parents' divorce, though I'm not sure it's fair to imply the correlation. Before the divorce they had fights about the fact that she wouldn't sell any of Papa's old belongings, or dispose of the boxes of paperwork, but it wasn't those fights or any other that finally broke them up so much as the way they had less and less to say to one another when they were happy. With my father out of the house, my mother threw herself into a mission to clear her grandfather's name, to finish in her lifetime what he hadn't been able to finish in his. There were no adults around to talk her out of it, only me. She asked me what I would do if someone told a lie about her, asked if she died with it still written down somewhere, whether I would ever give up fighting to prove the truth. I knew that the only correct answer was no.

Her odds of succeeding were low. When she started the process, it had been fifteen years since Papa's death, and more than seventy since the conviction. Still, there was a logic to her argument—the discharge paperwork she kept carbon copies of in our attic said he'd been pardoned, and she thought it would be easy, from there, to have his dishonorable discharge changed to an honorable one. It didn't make sense, she reasoned, that if he'd been cleared of the crime he was accused of, that the government should consider him dishonorable. As years passed without action or response, she was buoyed by occasional signs of what she saw as precedent on her side. In 1999, Lt. Henry Flipper, the first Black graduate of West Point, had been given a posthumous presidential pardon, more than a hundred years after he was falsely charged with embezzlement in a scandal designed to push him out of the service. My mother had bought a bottle of champagne and shared it with me while we watched the official pardon ceremony, where descendants of the late Lt. Flipper sat on a podium with Bill Clinton and Colin Powell and received a formal apology.

"Do you see what happens," my mother had asked me, "when you don't give up on making things right?"

But what I'd seen happen—before that brief moment of optimism and especially in the five years since—was my mother becoming increasingly dependent on an outcome that seemed less and less likely. She taught elementary school, but all of her holiday breaks, half days, and weekends went into the litigation, into letters to the army, the president, her congressman. Not counting our hourly labor, my mother must have already spent almost half of the $220,000 we were theoretically owed on court filing fees, photocopies, and certified letters. When I had lived at home, my spare time went into organizing the files, photo-copying important documents, holding my breath. Two months after I moved to Oakland, the Supreme Court denied my mother's request that they hear her appeal against the VA. My mother called from the other side of the country, sounding defeated. There was nobody left to argue with.

"Papa will never have his name back," she said.

"You know who he was," I said, but it didn't seem to comfort her any.

After I got off the phone with her, I'd felt helpless, and finally booked a reservation on one of the Alcatraz tour boats. When I got out to the docks at my appointed time, I couldn't bring myself to actually get on the boat. I'd milled around Fisherman's Wharf instead, ducking out of tourists' snapshots and trying to name the source of my unease. I'd watched the water for a while—the same fierce, unwavering blue of it that I felt had called me here—and ended up stopping at one of the gift shops on the pier and buying my mother a poster commemorating the Native American takeover of the island. Alcatraz Indians, it said on the front, under a cartoonish picture of something half man, half eagle. *I thought it might be easier to remember that this could also be a place of freedom,* I scrawled on the back. She never mentioned receiving it.

Reticence was not my mother's nature, and when, in the weeks that followed, she had less and less to say about anything, I panicked. She was still a few weeks away from the start of the school year. I insisted she come out to visit me. I wanted to see for myself how bad things were with her.

She arrived twenty pounds lighter than when I'd seen her a few months ago. My mother, who lived in discount denim and told me once that she found mascara unseemly, was wearing makeup and designer heels. If I hadn't known she didn't believe in mood-altering drugs, I would have taken her for heavily medicated. She was dressed like an actress auditioning for the part of my mother in a movie. A different daughter might have been reassured, but I looked at my mother and saw a person directing all of her energy toward being outwardly composed because the inside was a lost cause.

"How are you doing?" I asked her once we'd gotten back from the airport and settled her into my apartment.

"How do you think?" she asked.

I offered to sleep on the couch and give her the bedroom, but she refused, and most nights passed out on the couch by ten, after watching syndicated sitcoms and having two glasses of wine. When I'd imagined her having more time for normalcy when the case was over, I hadn't imagined this. Nothing I suggested excited or distracted her. When pressed, she made increasingly bizarre plans for the future. She was moving in with me, never mind that she had a house full of things on the other side of the country. She was moving to France, never mind that she didn't speak French. She was joining the Peace Corps, never mind that she was in her late forties and had never so much as been camping because she didn't understand why anyone would voluntarily separate themselves from reliable indoor plumbing.

It was probably my mother's focus on unlikely and unreasonable futures that gave me the idea that I could still fix something for her. I found Nancy Morton, who was technically my mother's first cousin, and, besides me, her last living relative. Nancy was Charlie Sullivan's granddaughter too, and my mother had not seen her since his funeral. The family's failure to bridge their divide in her generation was on her list of ways Papa's legacy was being dishonored.

I'd already made arrangements with Nancy and booked the boat tickets by the time I explained the plan to my mother. She was wary. She had tried to reach out to her cousins when the litigation first began and her letter had come back marked return to sender from the address she had for Nancy's older brother.

"They're still your family," I insisted.

"They are *not* my family," my mother said. "We're just related."

I'd finally convinced her that the whole trip was what her grandfather would have wanted for us, because I had her own words on my side. Almost immediately, I had doubts about the brilliance of my plan, but it was too late. I'd invited a group of practical strangers to meet us on a boat, and now here we were—instant family, just add water.

～

It was uncharacteristically hot for the Bay Area in August. The air felt thick and stifling like the East Coast summers I had left behind. Nancy Morton kept pulling an economy-size bottle of sunscreen out of her giant straw handbag and slathering gobs of it on her already reddening skin. Her husband, Ken, kept staring at his sneakers. He had barely spoken since we'd all done handshakes and introductions at the pier. Actually, he had spoken exactly six words since then, those words being "Kelli, put your damn clothes on," when their younger daughter had taken off her damp T-shirt and begun walking around in her bikini top. Their older daughter, Sarah, was twenty-three—we shared a birthday, though a year apart—and looked as embarrassed by her family as I was.

This was only the third time that my mother and Nancy had seen each other. When they were small children, Nancy and her brother had been brought to their grandparents' house for monthly visits, on the condition that my mother was out of the house. By six, my mother understood that she was Black and her family was not, and this was why the rule existed, but her understanding was impersonal and matter-of-fact; it was a rule like gravity, one from a higher authority. From the window of the neighbor's apartment where she'd been sent, my mother could see Nancy on the front steps of their grandparents' building. She was a small girl with a long blond braid hanging down her back; it brushed against the dingy ground as Nancy did her best to flatten a series of bottle caps with a rock. My mother was generally obedient, but her curiosity and her nagging sense that other children weren't sent away when their families came by got the best of her; while the neighbor who was supposed to be keeping an eye on her watched her stories in the bedroom, my mother went downstairs and peeked through the glass of the front door to get a better look at Nancy, who finally looked up and pressed her face against the other side of the glass to look back. My mother opened the door.

"Why were you watching me?" Nancy asked.

"We're cousins," said my mother. "And your hair looks pretend."

"Is not," said Nancy. "And I don't have cousins."

"Do too. I live here. With our Grammy and Papa."

The names meant nothing to Nancy, who called them Grandpa and Grandma Sullivan, but my mother offered as evidence the locket around her neck, the one with her grandparents' pictures sealed in it. It was convincing enough for Nancy, who shrieked and hugged her. Nancy offered her a flattened bottle cap, and when my mother said it looked like a coin, they got the idea to play store, make-believe buying and selling flowers and dirt from the backyard and the clothing and jewelry they were wearing. They were absorbed enough not to notice that Nancy's parents had emerged from the apartment and were on their way out until after Nancy's mother opened the front door and saw them playing together.

She screamed her daughter's name and grabbed Nancy by her pigtail, pulling her by her hair down the block to their car, Nancy's neck straining unnaturally backward the whole way. My mother, afraid Nancy's mother would come back for it, clutched the bottle cap in her hand so tightly that it sliced her skin. Nancy cried hysterically as her mother shoved her into the back seat and slammed the door, without a word to or from her husband, who took his son's hand, followed his wife and screaming daughter to the car, and started the engine without so much as saying goodbye. My mother watched them drive away like that, her own palm still bleeding. Nancy's tear-streaked face was pressed against the rear window. It was the last time her uncle brought his family over, the last time my mother saw him aside from his parents' funerals. For years she told and retold Papa the story of the game, as if she could find the detail that had made it go wrong, until she was old enough to understand that she was the detail, the wrong thing. *Someday,* Papa told her, *all this foolishness will be done, and all my grandchildren and their children will celebrate together.* But whatever it would take to make someday happen, it did not seem to be happening in her house.

"You have no idea how much you take for granted," my mother told me the first time I'd brought a white friend home to play. But she was wrong about that—you take nothing for granted when the price of it is etched across the face of the person you love the most, when you are born into a series of loans and know you will never be up to the cost of the debt.

∼

"Cecilia is studying to be a doctor," my mother told the Mortons as we waited for the ferry to depart. It wasn't true: I had a master's in public health, which my mother liked to think of as a stepping-stone to medical school rather than the beginning of a career in social work. When I told my father what I planned to do with my life, he told me not to blame him for the fact that I'd inherited my mother's enthusiasm for impractical causes, but he sent me the money for the plane ticket.

"A doctor," said Nancy. "That's impressive. Perhaps some of your drive will rub off on Sarah. She has it in her head to go traipsing around the desert for a year."

I looked at Sarah with real interest for the first time. She was rolling her eyes and twisting a strand of hair around her finger so tightly that her fingertips were turning red. We were built similarly, tits so that anything you wore that wasn't a giant burlap sack bordered on obscene, but the resemblance ended there. She'd made a pillow out of her Vanderbilt sweatshirt and was resting against it, dangling one arm over the back edge of her seat.

"Cecilia has always been good with science," my mother said. "She gets that from her father's side. I'd wanted to look you up for years, but it was Cecilia and her tech smarts that found you. I never had much of a head for science."

My mother was basing my scientific excellence on a ribbon I won for growing hydroponic tomatoes in the seventh grade, though I'd subsequently nearly failed biochemistry and dropped physics altogether. My father was a food critic who had recently been berated by a molecular gastronomist for identifying liquid nitrogen as "smoke" in his review. My tech smarts consisted of having entered Nancy Morton's older brother's name into Google. In fairness to my mother, we had, both of us, grown up without the ability to type someone's name into the ether and receive an immediate report on their current whereabouts. I'd always known about her cousins, but only that year had it occurred to me that one of the great unanswerable questions of her life was now in fact answerable, and instantly at that. The internet did still feel like a kind of mysterious magic then, a new power we had all only recently been granted and were still learning to use. When I finally left the Bay fifteen years later—the nonprofit I worked for was shutting down and I was already barely able to keep up with my rent increases—I took a long walk through the hills and looked across the water at the city that tech rebuilt and tried to remember when I'd first seen it coming, when I'd remembered that all magic, all progress, has a price.

Even at the time, the magic I used to get us answers had a trace of the ominous: it turned out that Nancy's brother had been killed in a car crash three years earlier. Nancy and her family had been mentioned in the obituary. I'd offered my belated condolences and invited them down to meet us on one of the Alcatraz ferries. They lived farther north, in Sonoma, and after a brief hesitation she had agreed to drive down for the day.

"Well it was different then," Nancy said. "With girls and science. They didn't encourage us much, did they, Anne?"

"No," said my mother. "No, they didn't. Lots of things were different then."

An unsaid thing hung in the air for a moment. Ken Morton cleared his throat.

"So," he asked, "why Alcatraz? Lovely day for it, but kind of an odd choice."

"I was going to ask the same thing. Interesting place for a reunion. We've never been—just moved out here a few years ago and never got around to half the tours. I hear it's beautiful though."

My mother looked like she might cry. Without thinking, I moved closer to her. It hadn't occurred to me to tell them why I had invited them here specifically. I had assumed that they would know.

"Didn't you know?" my mother asked. "That Papa was at Alcatraz? That that's why he—that's why things happened the way they did?"

A moment of surprise passed over Nancy's face, and then she collected herself.

"I had heard," she said slowly, "that he had done some time in prison, and was never really—never really right after that. I didn't know that it was Alcatraz. You know, I didn't get to know him that well. Not like you did."

"I guess you didn't," said my mother. "Nobody else did." My mother sat on one of the benches on deck and hugged her arms to her chest. I sat down beside her. I could tell she was trying not to cry. I put an arm around her and patted her shoulder gently. The Mortons looked embarrassed to be there, and then turned away to watch San Francisco disappear from view.

~

Here is what you have to understand about my mother's childhood: it wasn't one. Her mother was the younger of Charlie and Louise's two children, both raised on the see-saw of his impractical excesses and her Yankee frugality. At sixteen, my grandmother ran off to join a theater; two years later she came back with a Black baby. She stayed home long enough to leave my mother in her parents' care and to meet a traveling salesman whom she ran off with a few months later. They never heard from her again. Some years later, the salesman sent a note with a copy of her obituary attached. When my mother was small, she and Papa would sit and make up stories about all the places her mother might be. Infinityland: somewhere north of Kansas, a place where you kept going and going but could never leave because it was always getting bigger. Elfworld: somewhere in West Florida, where they kept shrinking you and shrinking you and you didn't realize you were an elf too until it was too late to do anything about it.

For years they lived together in the imaginary places, a world you could only be kept from by enchantment, but as soon as she was old enough, my mother left and kept going too, left that house and let the business of loving the man who raised her be confined to telephone calls from faraway places. It was a decision that probably saved her life, and one for which she never forgave herself. I didn't—and still don't—dare compare the terms of my life to my mother's, the stakes of my choices to hers, but I understand more now about how it feels to love the excess in people, about how knowing someone else's love will consume you doesn't make it any less real or any less reciprocated, about how you can leave a person behind just to save the thing they value most—yourself. Or maybe I understood it even then but couldn't have told you how.

∼

Here is what you have to understand about Charlie Sullivan: his life at home as a child was bad enough that joining the army at the tail end of World War I seemed like a safer and more cheerful alternative. At fifteen he falsified his birth certificate and enlisted. A captain decided he was too scrawny to be sent overseas. Instead, he was stationed as a border guard, where he spent his days looking backward toward California because his orders were to shoot anyone coming from Mexico, and he figured he couldn't shoot anyone if he didn't see them. They'd given him a gun that didn't work right anyway; it stuck sometimes when he tried to fire, which at first struck him as fortuitous. When it occurred to him that it might also be dangerous, he complained to a commanding officer, who told him if he wanted a real gun, he'd have to be a real soldier.

Stop complaining, they said, and so he did, until the night he was cleaning his gun and it fired accidentally, putting the same bullet through his best friend and an officer who'd been standing in the doorway. It had happened that quickly, the blast of the gun catching his friend in mid-laugh, then silencing the commanding officer's scream. The first men to arrive at the scene had found Charlie sobbing over the body of his best friend, a nineteen-year-old kid from Jersey who wanted to be an architect. It wasn't until the base commander showed up that anyone even suggested he'd done it on purpose, but as soon as he did, Charlie was led off in handcuffs, and the previous reports of his gun malfunctioning vanished. They sent him to Alcatraz where he was convicted and sentenced to death by firing squad. They dragged him out of the basement for his execution twice, only to find it had been stalled. His appointed lawyer, an old army man who thought he'd seen enough evil to know what it wasn't, wouldn't retire until he got Charlie Sullivan out of prison. He managed to get sworn statements about my great-grandfather's faulty gun, his temperament and friendship with the deceased, the medical report that concluded one bullet had killed both men. It was enough to get him pardoned, though he was still dishonorably discharged. The army would admit only to procedural error.

When my mother left, he was alone with his ghosts. He didn't have my mother's patience for strategic approaches, didn't go through all the proper channels. He called and wrote letters to the Pentagon, trying to get his dishonorable discharge changed to an honorable one, trying to get the veterans' benefits he'd been demanding for forty years, trying to get a person instead of letterhead to answer him. He wrote to whom it may concern, but it concerned no one. When at last he got a personal response, a *We are very sorry but no*, from a Maj. Johnson somewhere, he dressed himself in a uniform he'd bought from an army surplus store, stood in the living room, and shot himself in the head.

My mother was a junior in college then, already engaged to my father. She spent money they had saved for her wedding to have him buried properly. It was nothing glitzy, no velvet and mahogany, but there was a coffin and a church service. My mother and a sprinkling of neighbors came to pay their last respects. Nancy's father was shamed into his Sunday best. He brought his children, including Nancy, but not his wife. They sat on the opposite side of a half-empty church. They didn't speak.

$\sim$

When I am angry at my mother sometimes, I tell myself this story. If you really want to know what the six of us were doing on a boat to Alcatraz, here is what you need to understand about me: at eighteen I'd joined a college literary club, whereupon we came up with the brilliant idea of tattooing ourselves with quotations from our favorite authors. Mine says *The past isn't dead. It isn't even past.* Growing up I watched my mother's every strategic move with some mixture of awe and resentment. I watched her stand up to lawyers who were better dressed and better paid, to imposing men in uniform, to friends who begged her to let the whole thing go already. I wondered sometimes where she got the strength for battle after battle, but more often than not she answered my question for me. After setbacks it was my comfort she sought, my hand she held, and for every word of encouragement I gave her I found myself swallowing the bitter declaration that I had never signed up for any of this—not the paperwork, not the support, not the faith in the ultimate benevolence of the universe that she seemed to take for granted that I shared with her. And yet, faith like that is contagious: I greeted her plans to spend the money she thought was coming to us by donating a bench in her grandfather's name to the city park with the wary reminder that we had no money coming to us yet; still I pictured him smiling down at us as we sat on it, the first generation in the family to achieve some semblance of peace. I rolled my eyes at my mother's occasional fantasy of being sought out by her missing cousins, but I memorized their names in case I ever ran into them, regularly looked over my shoulder and peered into the faces of strangers to see if I could map out any family resemblance.

Looking at them on the boat I'd summoned them to, I realized I never would have known them by sight; they looked like any other strangers. After my mother's revelation, the gulf between our families seemed even bigger than it had been when we'd met at the pier. The Mortons didn't talk much the whole rest of the boat ride, not even to each other. I sat by my mother and kept rubbing her shoulder.

"This could still work out," I said, even though I didn't know anymore what was supposed to be working.

$\sim$

Alcatraz loomed over us all, stony and angular with patches of green. My mother made halting conversation with Nancy. A woman in front of us pointed enthusiastically at the military barracks ahead. I looked up—rows and rows of matching windows, peeling paint that might have been white once. An old US penitentiary sign had been affixed to the building over the welcome indians graffiti that no one had painted over. All that history, bleeding into itself in the wrong order. Sarah was standing beside me, focused on the same sign. She fished through her shoulder bag and emerged with a tin of mints; I took one when she offered it and chewed, feeling the little bits of blue crystal grind against my teeth.

"Would you mind telling me what the hell is going on here?" she asked.

"At this point your guess is as good as mine," I said.

"I thought this was going to be a joke or something," Sarah continued. "I mean, who has long-lost relatives anymore?"

"Didn't you know about us?" I asked. I had known about them for as long as I could remember.

"Not really. My mom was never that close to her parents. We saw them like every other Thanksgiving. Less than that once my uncle died. And then they died too. We don't really even talk about them that much. Mom's been weird lately. I think she was happy to get the call. Dad thinks this whole thing is a bad idea. FYI, he thinks you're going to ask for money or something."

"Oh," I said. "Well we're not."

"Didn't think so." She stopped to examine a purple flower on a bush, then snapped it off and twisted it between her fingers, staining them lavender. "My mom said something about a lawsuit."

"It's over. And anyway, it was never about the money. It was about the fact that he never should have been here."

I told her the story my mother had told me, the faulty gun, the death of his friends, the rats, his suicide.

"Fuck," she said, and we were quiet the rest of the way up.

∼

When we caught up with our parents, I found my mother still listing slightly exaggerated versions of my accomplishments. It was the kind of subtle inflation of the truth you'd find in a family's annual holiday newsletter, but it made me angry. It wasn't that I doubted she was proud of me—her faith in me, I knew, was boundless. It was their faith in me she didn't trust, and I didn't like it, the way a group of strangers had the power to shake my mother's confidence. I had orchestrated the visit confident that my mother's cousin would be grateful for the chance to make amends, that she and her family would be eager to prove themselves better than the people who raised her. It had honestly not occurred to me that my mother and I would have to make a case for ourselves, that conditions could possibly be such that we were the ones who were supposed to impress them.

"You don't have to treat them like they're visiting royalty," I muttered to my mother as we approached the entrance of the main prison building. "They're just people."

"I'm treating them like they're people. They aren't props, Cecilia. You can't just order them to show up and expect the rest to take care of itself. But don't worry, keep up the attitude and no amount of convincing will make them like you. Be exactly what they were expecting, if that makes you happy."

I sulked behind my mother as we collected our headphones and prepared for the tour. The main prison building was dim, dingy, with anachronistically fresh green and gray paint. We walked into a room of mock visiting windows, glass with holes cut out for human contact. A small girl in pink overalls sat at one of the windows, tapping the glass and frowning at the dead black telephone she held against her ear, seeming genuinely confused by the absence of a voice on the other end. My mother took a breath and walked through the entryway. Rows and rows of prison bars greeted us. A family in front of us stretched out their souvenir map and tried to locate Al Capone's cell. I put one side of my headset over my ear and let the other headphone rest just behind the other ear, in case I needed to hear something more interesting. What I heard was Kelli.

"*Eewwwww*," she said to the exposed cell toilet, littered with tourist trash: cigarette butts and crumpled pieces of paper.

"Shut up and stop being an idiot, Kelli," said Sarah, which I appreciated until it was silent because no one could think of anything to say that wasn't idiotic. I put both headphones over my ears. *You are entitled to food, clothing, shelter, and medical attention. Everything else is a privilege.* I examined a scuff mark on the floor, noted how many people must have walked over this same ground, paid for the luxury of being reminded what privileges were. I tried to imagine what it would be like to live underneath it. *Turn left to see the gun gallery,* my audio guide informed me, then provided me with the sound of a smattering of rifle fire *rat-a-tat-tat,* in case, I suppose, I didn't know what a gun was.

I did know, and I knew my mother did too, knew she'd replayed Papa's last minutes over and over again in her head. I had sat with her when she woke up screaming from nightmares about it, or from the old nightmare, the one she inherited from him, the bullet flying from his gun, ripping through his bunkmate, going straight through whoever else appeared in the dream and tried to stop it. She kept the gun he shot himself with. It was locked in a case in our basement somewhere, unloaded. I had my own nightmares sometimes. I slept quietly, but not well. Lately I'd been dreaming I got a phone call like my mother had. I'd been having her nightmare, only this time it was her with the gun to her head, and I never woke up in time to save her.

Nothing was working out the way I'd wanted it to. Ken Morton was still walking around with his hands in his pockets, looking like he'd rather be anywhere else. Nancy Morton and my mother were still making tentative small talk about Sarah and Kelli and me and the weather. Kelli had surreptitiously placed her iPod earbuds under the audio tour headphones and was humming a pop song and making eyes at a spiky-haired boy who was taking the tour with his family. Sarah had pulled out a notebook. I tried to peer over her shoulder to read it, but her handwriting was illegible. No one was taking this seriously enough. Even the site itself seemed like a cheap approximation of the sacred ground I'd been expecting. It was more national park than anything else, dozens of people with sunglasses in their pockets clutching souvenir photos of themselves in the mock gallows and checking their watches to make sure they had left enough time for a picnic lunch. *Loud talking, shouting, whistling, singing, or other unnecessary noises are prohibited,* said the automated tour guide. I took my headphones off altogether. Kids ran by, giggling, their parents calling after them. A group of women in matching purple sun visors kept loudly asking questions of one another although it was clear none of them knew the answers.

My mother paused in front of one of the restored jail cells, and the rest of us stopped behind her. She slid the headphones off of her ears and walked in. Nancy followed her. Even with just the two of them, it was crowded, but Sarah and I squeezed in behind them anyway. Under the circumstances, neither of us quite trusted our mothers to their own devices.

"Tight squeeze," said Nancy. "Can you even imagine living in here?"

My mother opened and shut her mouth, but no words came out. I could see in her eyes the first of the tears I'd been expecting since she'd lost the appeal, the practiced composure of the past few weeks slipping from her. She sat on the floor of the cell and began to weep, shielding her perfectly made-up face with her hands. Ken Morton, who was still standing awkwardly outside the cell gate, took Kelli's hand and led her away. I tried to push past Nancy to sit beside my mother and hold her hand, but Nancy sat down beside her first, and let her cry. Sarah tugged at my sleeve, but I didn't go anywhere. I felt that the whole escapade was my mistake, and I'd be damned if I was going to let my mother's family screw her up again on my watch.

"That was stupid of me," said Nancy. She put a hand on my mother's shoulder. "Of course you've imagined."

My mother had stopped crying, but she didn't respond.

"I wanted to say something, you know," said Nancy. "At the funeral. I saw you sitting by yourself and I knew right away who you were, and I wanted to speak."

"But you didn't," said my mother, the edge I'd missed in her since she'd arrived in San Francisco finally creeping back into her voice. "You didn't even say hello."

"I was young," she said.

"I was younger," said my mother. "You were the only family I had left when he died. I thought his reputation would matter to you, like it did to me. He was your grandfather too."

"Not in the same way he was yours," said Nancy. "And I can't change that. It took me years to understand why my mother reacted to you the way she did, and when I did, I was ashamed, but I was still her daughter. There was a lot of sorting out to do. I do think she changed some. I think she regretted some of it. I know I did."

"At least you know what you regret. I'm forty-seven years old and after everything, Cecilia is all I've got."

"That's not true," I said, even though I had believed it all my life.

"Sometimes I think I know how Papa felt—I mean," she said, noting my alarm, "not that I'd ever want to end it the way he did. Just that I don't know what there is left to try."

I looked at the metal bars, the scratches and fingerprints on them, the open doorway on the other side. How easy it was to feel stuck; how easy it was to walk out.

"There's this," Sarah said finally.

"There's this," my mother repeated, in a voice somewhere between a laugh and a sob. From farther down the hall, tourists were gawking at us. Nancy wrapped a protective arm around my mother, who leaned into her shoulder. Sarah grabbed my arm as she stepped away, and I walked out with her, accepting that it was time to let our mothers cry. I was unaccustomed to that then—to leaving while my mother was in need of comfort, to trusting anyone else to know what to do. I let myself be led away because Sarah seemed confident it was possible.

In the museum store, Kelli was laughing and dangling a pair of souvenir handcuffs just out of reach of the spiky-haired boy. Ken Morton was outside already, smoking a cigarette. He nodded in our general direction and went back to his smoking. This, I thought, was one of those times it would be easier to be male, or a smoker, to have a ready excuse to remove myself from emotional proceedings without anyone making an issue of it. Sarah pulled the mints out of her purse again and offered me one. She kept snapping the container open and shut.

"Mom hasn't been the same since my uncle died," said Sarah. "It wasn't even that they were super close, just that he was what she had in the world, you know? Kelli is a godawful pain in the ass, but if anything happened to her, I'd be a wreck. I think that was why she was so excited to meet your mom. She liked the idea of having more family again. It might be good, if they can be friends."

"If," I said.

"It could happen," said Sarah. "Nothing like a prison to give you faith in humanity."

"A prison with a souvenir penny press," I said.

I looked around at all of the things for sale. Chocolate bars in Alcatraz wrapping. Posters with blown-up versions of prison regulations: #21. WORK. YOU ARE REQUIRED TO WORK AT WHATEVER YOU ARE TOLD TO DO. Along the wall a row of bronze cast keys were each engraved with cell numbers. I lifted one up with my finger for Sarah to see.

"Who buys these?" I asked. "Who walks in here and says this, this is what I need?"

"People who don't know what they need in the first place," she said. "So, pretty much anybody."

I considered this. I wondered how much I'd have to steal for it to equal $227,035.87. It seemed strange to me to have the number in my head then, and though it would never stop seeming strange to me, I kept the running tally for years after that afternoon, did the math annually, out of habit, even after my mother had stopped requesting it, even after I had stopped thinking of the world as a place that kept track of what it owed people, even after I stopped thinking of myself as a person who had the power to make demands of the world and learned to be a person who came up with her own small daily answers like everyone else. There was something comforting about imagining I knew exactly what I'd been cheated out of.

When my mother and Nancy emerged into the gift shop, their eyes were dry. There was something girlish in the way my mother came over to me, lighter after the cathartic tears. I tapped a key absentmindedly and it bumped the others; they jingled like wind chimes.

"We missed the three o'clock ferry," I told her.

"Did we?" she said, ruffling her fingers through my hair. "I think we'll live, kiddo. Let's hang out for a while."

I watched her walk out with Nancy Morton. The sun was hazy and insistent, and everyone seemed to shimmer as they stepped outside. I watched them walk away, and I had the feeling I was watching something heavy miraculously float.

In the years that followed, we would try two more holidays with the Mortons before the efforts were suspended indefinitely, victim to all of us being busy and, frankly, happier on our own. When we were alone after the final visit, my mother would confide in me that after all that, Nancy

Morton had grown up to be boring. When my mother accepted that the legal system wouldn't give her justice, she said she would write a book about Papa's story, and while I heard about it for years, I never saw a manuscript. Sarah and I began a correspondence that started earnest and effusive, but tapered off, until eventually the extent of our relationship was me clicking like on her family photographs, not remembering which of her children was named what, her once commenting "Congratulations, I must have missed this!" when I was tagged in a photograph with two of the children I worked with, me intending but never bothering to correct her assumption they were mine.

That afternoon at Alcatraz we were all together, and I didn't know whether I had managed anything good or permanent or healing in gathering us there, only that it had previously been impossible. I slipped a bronze key off of its hook and closed it into my palm. I wanted someone to stop me or I wanted someone to tell me it was mine. I squeezed the key into my palm and walked out without anyone noticing. I walked into the glare of the light, down to the picnic tables near the water, where my family was gathered and laughing. I called to Sarah. I held the key out in my open palm and went to show my cousin what I'd done.

AT THE ROUND EARTH' S IMAGINED CORNERS

LAUREN GROFF
2022 JOYCE CAROL OATES PRIZE RECIPIENT

Jude was born in a Cracker-style house at the edge of a swamp that boiled
with unnamed species of reptiles. Few people lived in the center of Florida
then. Air-conditioning was for the rich, and the rest compensated with
high ceilings, sleeping porches, attic fans. Jude's father was a herpetologist
at the university, and if snakes hadn't slipped their way into their hot house,
his father would have filled it with them anyway. Coils of rattlers sat in
formaldehyde on the windowsills. Writhing knots of reptiles lived in the
coops out back, where his mother had once tried to raise chickens. At an
early age, Jude learned to keep a calm heart when touching fanged things.
He was barely walking when his mother came into the kitchen to find
a coral snake chasing its red and yellow tail around his wrist. His father
was watching from across the room, laughing. His mother was a Yankee,
a Presbyterian. She was always weary; she battled the house's mold and
humidity and devilish reek of snakes without help. His father wouldn't
allow a black person through his doors, and they didn't have the money to
hire a white woman. Jude's mother was afraid of scaly creatures, and sang
hymns in the attempt to keep them out. When she was pregnant with Jude's
sister, she came into the bathroom to take a cool bath one August night
and, without her glasses, missed the three-foot albino alligator her husband
had stored in the bathtub. The next morning, she was gone. She returned a
week later. And after Jude's sister was born dead, a perfect petal of a baby,
his mother never stopped singing under her breath.

~

Noise of the war grew louder. At last, it became impossible to ignore.
Jude was two. His mother pressed his father's new khaki suit and then

Jude's father's absence filled the house with a kind of cool breeze. He was flying cargo planes in France. Jude thought of scaly creatures flapping great wings midair, his father angrily riding.

While Jude napped the first day they were alone in the house, his mother tossed all of the jars of dead snakes into the swamp and neatly beheaded the living ones with a hoe. She bobbed her hair with gardening shears. Within a week, she had moved them ninety miles to the beach. When she thought he was asleep on the first night in the new house, she went down to the water's edge in the moonlight and screwed her feet into the sand. It seemed that the glossed edge of the ocean was chewing her up to her knees. Jude held his breath, anguished. One big wave rolled past her shoulders, and when it receded, she was whole again.

This was a new world, full of dolphins that slid up the coastline in shining arcs. Jude loved the wedges of pelicans ghosting overhead, the mad dig after periwinkles that disappeared deeper into the wet sand. He kept count in his head when they hunted for them, and when they came home, he told his mother that they had dug up four hundred and sixty-one. She looked at him unblinking behind her glasses and counted the creatures aloud. When she finished, she washed her hands for a long time at the sink.

You like numbers, she said at last, turning around.

Yes, he said. And she smiled, and a kind of gentle shine came from her that startled him. He felt it seep into him, settle in his bones. She kissed him on the crown and put him to bed, and when he woke in the middle of the night to find her next to him, he tucked his hand under her chin, where it stayed until morning.

∼

He began to sense that the world worked in ways beyond him, that he was only grasping at threads of a greater fabric. Jude's mother started a bookstore. Because women couldn't buy land in Florida for themselves, his uncle, a roly-poly little man who looked nothing like Jude's father, bought the store with her money and signed the place over to her. His mother began wearing suits that showed her décolletage and taking her glasses off before boarding the streetcars, so that the eyes she turned to the public were soft. Instead of singing Jude to sleep as she had in the snake house, she read to him. She read Shakespeare, Neruda, Rilke, and he fell asleep with their cadences and the sea's slow rhythm entwined in his head.

Jude loved the bookstore; it was a bright place that smelled of new paper. Lonely war brides came with their prams and left with an armful of Modern Library classics, sailors on leave wandered in only to exit, charmed, with sacks of books pressed to their chests. After-hours, his mother would turn off the lights and open the back door to the black folks who waited patiently there, the dignified man in his watch cap who loved Galsworthy, the fat woman who worked as a maid and read a novel every day. Your father would squeal. Well, foo on him, his mother said to Jude, looking so fierce she erased the last traces in his mind of the tremulous woman she'd been.

~

One morning just before dawn, he was alone on the beach when he saw a vast metallic breaching a hundred yards offshore. The submarine looked at him with its single periscope eye and slipped silently under again. Jude told nobody. He kept this dangerous knowledge inside him, where it tightened and squeezed, but where it couldn't menace the greater world.

~

Jude's mother brought in a black woman named Sandy to help her with housework and to watch Jude while she was at the store. Sandy and his mother became friends, and some nights he would awaken to laughter from the veranda and come out to find his mother and Sandy in the night breeze off the ocean. They drank sloe gin fizzes and ate lemon cake, which Sandy was careful to keep on hand even though by then sugar was getting scarce. They let him have a slice, and he'd fall asleep on Sandy's broad lap, sweetness souring on his tongue, and in his ears the exhalation of the ocean, the sound of women's voices.

At six, he discovered multiplication all by himself, crouched over an anthill in the hot sun. If twelve ants left the anthill per minute, he thought, that meant seven hundred twenty departures per hour, an immensity of leaving, of return. He ran into the bookstore, wordless with happiness.

When he buried his head in his mother's lap, the women chatting with her at the counter mistook his sobbing for something sad.

I'm sure the boy misses his father, one lady said, intending to be kind.

No, his mother said. She alone understood his bursting heart and scratched his scalp gently. But something shifted in Jude; and he thought with wonder of his father, of whom his mother had spoken so rarely in all these years that the man himself had faded. Jude could barely recall the rasp of scale on scale and the darkness of the Cracker house in the swamp, curtains closed to keep out the hot, stinking sun.

~

But it was as if the well-meaning lady had summoned him, and Jude's father came home. He sat, immense and rough-cheeked, in the middle of the sunroom. Jude's mother sat nervously opposite him on the divan, angling her knees away from his. The boy played quietly with his wooden train on the floor. Sandy came in with fresh cookies, and when she went back into the kitchen, his father said something so softly Jude couldn't catch it. His mother stared at his father for a long time, then got up and went to the kitchen, and the screen door slapped, and the boy never saw Sandy again.

While his mother was gone, Jude's father said, We're going home.

Jude couldn't look at his father. The space in the air where he existed was too heavy and dark. He pushed his train around the ankle of a chair. Come here, his father said, and slowly, the boy stood and went to his father's knee.

A big hand flicked out, and Jude's face burned from ear to mouth. He fell down but didn't cry out. He sucked in blood from his nose and felt it pool behind his throat.

His mother ran in and picked him up. What happened? she shouted, and his father said in his cold voice, Boy's timid. Something's wrong with him.

He keeps things in. He's shy, said his mother, and carried Jude away. He could feel her trembling as she washed the blood from his face. His father came into the bathroom and she said through her teeth, Don't you ever touch him again.

He said, I won't have to.

His mother lay beside Jude until he fell asleep, but he woke to the moon through the automobile's windshield and his parents' jagged profiles staring ahead into the tunnel of the dark road.

∿

The house by the swamp filled with snakes again. The uncle who had helped his mother with the bookstore was no longer welcome, although he was the only family his father had. Jude's mother cooked a steak and potatoes every night but wouldn't eat. She became a bone, a blade. She sat in her housedress on the porch rocker, her hair slick with sweat. Jude stood near her and spoke the old sonnets into her ear. She pulled him to her side and put her face between his shoulder and neck, and when she blinked, her wet eyelashes tickled him, and he knew not to move away.

His father had begun, on the side, selling snakes to zoos and universities. He vanished for two, three nights in a row, and returned with clothes full of smoke and sacks of rattlers and blacksnakes. He'd been gone for two nights when his mother packed her blue cardboard suitcase with Jude's things on one side and hers on the other. She said nothing, but gave herself away with humming. They walked together over the dark roads and sat waiting for the train for a long time. The platform was empty; theirs was the last train before the weekend. She handed him caramels to suck, and he felt her whole body tremble through the thigh he pressed hard against hers.

So much had built up in him while they waited that it was almost a relief when the train came sighing into the station. His mother stood and reached for Jude. He smiled up into her soft answering smile.

Then Jude's father stepped into the lights and scooped him up. His body under Jude's was taut, and Jude was so surprised that the shout caught in his throat. His mother did not look at her husband or her son. She seemed a statue, thin and pale.

At last, when the conductor said, All aboard! she gave an awful strangled sound and rushed through the train's door. The train hooted and slowly moved off. Jude could now shout, and did, as loudly as he could, although his father held him too firmly to escape, but the train vanished his mother into the darkness without stopping.

∿

Then they were alone, Jude's father and he, in the house by the swamp.

Language wilted between them. Jude was the one who took up the sweeping and scrubbing, who made their sandwiches for supper. When his father was gone, he'd open the windows to let out some of the reptile rot. His father ripped up his mother's lilies and roses and planted mandarins and blueberries, saying that fruit brought birds and birds brought snakes. The boy walked three miles to school, where he told nobody that he already knew numbers better than the teachers did. He was small, but no one messed with him. On his first day, when a big ten-year-old tried to sneer at his clothes, Jude leapt at him with a viciousness he'd learned from watching rattlesnakes, and made the big boy's head bleed. The others avoided him. He was an in-between creature, motherless but not fatherless, stunted and ratty like a poor boy, but a professor's son, always correct with answers when the teachers called on him, but never offering a word on his own. The others kept their distance. Jude played by himself or with one of the succession of puppies that his father brought home. Inevitably, the dogs would run down to the edge of the swamp, and one of the fourteen- or fifteen-foot alligators would get them.

Jude's loneliness grew, became a living creature that shadowed him and wandered off only when he was in the company of his numbers. More than marbles or tin soldiers, they were his playthings. More than sticks of candy or plums, they made his mouth water. As messy as the world was, the numbers, predictable and polite, brought order.

~

When he was ten, a short, round man stopped him on the street and pushed a brown-paper package into his arms. Jude found him vaguely familiar but couldn't place him. The man pressed a finger to his lips, minced away. At home in his room at night, Jude unwrapped the books. One was a collection of Frost's poems. The other was a book of geometry, the world whittled down until it became a series of lines and angles. He looked up and morning was sunshot through the laurel oaks. More than the feeling that the book had taught him geometry was the feeling that it had showed the boy something that had been living inside him, undetected until now.

There was also a letter. It was addressed to him in his mother's round hand. When he sat in school dividing the hours until he could be free, when he made the supper of tuna sandwiches, when he ate with his father, who conducted to Benny Goodman on the radio, when he brushed his teeth and put on pajamas far too small for him, the four perfect right angles of the letter called to him. He put it under his pillow, unopened. For a week, the letter burned under everything, the way the sun on a hot, overcast day was hidden but always present.

At last, having squeezed everything to know out of the geometry book, he put the still-sealed envelope inside and taped up the covers and hid it between his mattress and box spring. He checked it every night after saying his prayers and was comforted into sleep. When, one night, he saw the book was untaped and the letter gone, he knew his father had found it and nothing could be done.

The next time he saw the little round man on the street, he stopped him. Who are you? he asked, and the man blinked and said, Your uncle. When no comprehension passed over the boy's face, the man threw his arms up and said, Oh, honey! and made as if to hug him, but Jude had already turned away.

～

Inexorably, the university grew. It swelled and expanded under a steady supply of conditioned air, swallowing the land between it and the swamp until the university's roads were built snug against his father's land. Dinners, now, were full of his father's invective: Did the university not know that his snakes needed a home, that this expanse of sandy acres was one of the richest reptile havens in North America? He would never sell, never. He would kill to keep it.

While his father spoke, the traitor in Jude dreamed of the sums his father had been offered. So simple, it seemed, to make the money grow. Unlike other kinds of numbers, money was already self-fertilized; it would double and double again until at last it made a roiling mass. If you had enough of it, Jude knew, nobody would ever have to worry again.

～

When Jude was thirteen, he discovered the university library. One summer day, he looked up from the pile of books he'd been contentedly digging through—trigonometry, statistics, calculus, whatever he could find—to see his father opposite him. Jude didn't know how long he'd been there. It was a humid morning, and even in the library the air was stifling, but his father looked leathered, cool in his sun-beaten shirt and red neckerchief.

Come on, then, he said. Jude followed, feeling ill. They rode in the pickup for two hours before Jude understood that they were going snaking together. This was his first time. When he was smaller, he'd begged to go, but every time, his father had said no, it was too dangerous, and Jude never argued that letting a boy live for a week alone in a house full of venom and guns and questionable wiring was equally unsafe.

His father pitched the tent and they ate beans from a can in the darkness. They lay side by side in their sleeping bags until his father said, You're good at math.

Jude said, I am, though with such understatement that it felt like a lie. Something shifted between them, and they fell asleep to a silence that was softer at its edges.

His father woke Jude before dawn and he stumbled out of the tent to grainy coffee with condensed milk and hot hush puppies. His father was after moccasins, and he gave Jude his waders and trudged through the swamp protected only by jeans and boots. He'd been bitten so often, he said, it had become routine. When he handed his son the stick and gestured at a black slash sunning on a rock, the boy had to imagine the snake as a line in space, only connecting point to point, to be able to grasp it. The snake spun from the number one to the number three to a defeated eight, and he deposited it in the sack. They worked in silence, only the noise of exuberant natural Florida filling their ears, the unafraid birds, the seethe of insects.

When Jude climbed back up into the truck at the end of the day, his legs shook from the effort it took him to be brave. So now you know, his father said in a strange, holy voice, and Jude was too tired to take the steps necessary then, and ever afterward until he was his father's own age, to understand.

$\sim$

His father began storing the fodder mice in Jude's closet, and to avoid the doomed squeaks, Jude joined the high school track team. He found his talent in the two-hundred-twenty-yard hurdles. When he came home with a trophy from the state games, his father held the trophy for a moment, then put it down.

Different if Negroes were allowed to run, he said.

Jude said nothing, and his father said, Lord knows I'm no lover of the race, but your average Negro could outrun any white boy I know.

Jude again said nothing, but avoided his father and didn't make him an extra steak when he cooked himself dinner. He still wasn't talking to him when his father went on an overnight trip and didn't come back for a week. Jude was used to it, and didn't get alarmed until the money ran out and his father still hadn't come home.

He alerted the secretary at the university, who sent out a group of graduate students to where Jude's father had been seen. They found the old man in his tent, bloated, his tongue protruding from a face turned black; and Jude understood then how even the things you loved most could kill you. He stored this knowledge in his bones and thought of it with every decision he made from then on.

At the funeral, out of a twisted loyalty to his father, he avoided his uncle. He didn't know if his mother knew she'd been widowed; he thought probably not. He told nobody at school that his father had died. He thought of himself as an island in the middle of the ocean, with no hope of seeing another island in the distance, or even a ship passing by.

～

Jude lived alone in the house. He let the mice die, then tossed the snakes in high twisting parabolas into the swamp. He scrubbed the house until it gleamed and the stench of reptiles was gone, then applied beeswax, paint, polish until it was a house fit for his mother. He waited. She didn't come.

The day he graduated from high school, Jude packed his clothes and sealed up the house and took the train to Boston. He'd heard from his uncle that his mother lived there, and so he'd applied and been accepted to college in the city. She owned a bookstore on a small, dark street. It took Jude a month of slow passing to gather the courage to go in. She was either in the back, or shelving books, or smiling in conversation with somebody, and he'd have a swim of darkness in his gut and know that it was fate telling him that today was not the day. When he went in, it was only because she was alone at the register, and her face—pouchy, waxy—was so sad in repose that the sight of it washed all thought from his head.

She rose with a wordless cry and flew to him. He held her stoically. She smelled like cats, and her clothes flopped on her as if she'd lost a lot of weight quickly. He told her about his father dying, and she nodded and said, I know, honey, I dreamed it.

She wouldn't let him leave her. She dragged him home with her and made him spaghetti carbonara and put clean sheets on the couch for him. Her three cats yowled under the door to her bedroom until she came back in with them. In the middle of the night, he woke to find her in her easy chair, clutching her hands, staring at him with glittering eyes. He closed his own and squeezed his hands into fists. He lay stiffly, almost shouting with the agony of being watched.

He went to see her once a week but refused all dinner invitations. He couldn't bear the density or lateness of her love. He was in his junior year when her long-percolating illness overcame her and she, too, left him. Now he was alone.

~

There was nothing but numbers then.

Later, there would be numbers but also the great ravishing machine in the laboratory into which Jude fed punched slips of paper and the motorcycle he rode because it roared like murder. He had been given a class to teach, but it was taken away after a month and he was told that he was better suited for research. In his late twenties, there were drunk and silly girls he could seduce without saying a word, because they felt a kind of danger coiled in him.

He rode his motorcycle too fast over icy roads. He swam at night in bays where great whites had been spotted. He bombed down ski slopes with only a hazy idea of the mechanics of snow. He drank so many beers he woke one morning to discover he'd developed a paunch as big as a pregnant woman's belly. He laughed to shake it, liked its wobble. It felt comforting, a child's pillow clutched to his midsection all day long.

By the time he was thirty, Jude was weary. He became drawn to bridges, their tensile strength, the cold river flowing underneath. A resolution was forming under his thoughts, like a contusion hardening under the skin.

And then he was crossing a road, and he hadn't looked first, and a bread truck, filled with soft dinner rolls so yeasty and warm that they were still expanding in their trays, hit him. He woke with a leg twisted beyond recognition, a mouth absent of teeth on one side, and his head in the lap of a woman who was crying for him, though she was a stranger, and he was bleeding all over her skirt, and there were warm mounds of bread scattered around them. It was the bread that made the pain return to his body, the deep warmth and good smell. He bit the hem of the woman's skirt to keep from screaming.

She rode with him to the hospital and stayed all night to keep him from falling asleep and possibly going into a coma. She was homely, three years older than he, a thick-legged antiques dealer who described her shop down a street so tiny the sun never touched her windows. He thought of her in the silent murky shop, swimming from credenza to credenza. She fed him rice pudding when she came to visit him in the hospital, and carefully brushed his wild hair until it was flat on his crown.

One night he woke with a jerk: the stars were angrily bright in the hospital window and someone in the room was breathing. There was a weight on his chest, and when he looked down, he found the woman's sleeping head. For a moment, he didn't know who she was. By the time he identified her, the feeling of unknowing had burrowed in. He would never know her; knowledge of another person was ungraspable, a cloud. He would never begin to hold another in his mind like an equation, pure and entire. He focused on the part of her thin hair, which in the darkness and closeness looked like inept stitches in white wax. He stared at the part until the horror faded, until her smell, the bitterness of unwashed hair, the lavender soap she used on her face, rose to him, and he put his nose against her warmth and inhaled her.

At dawn, she woke. Her cheek was creased from the folds in his gown. She looked at him wildly and he laughed, and she rubbed the drool from the corner of her mouth and turned away as if disappointed. He married her because to not do so had ceased to be an option during the night.

~

While he was learning how to walk again, he had a letter from the university down in Florida that made a tremendous offer for his father's land.

And so, instead of the honeymoon trip to the Thousand Islands, pines and cold water and his wife's bikini pressing into the dough of her flesh, they took a sleeping train down to Florida and walked in the heat to the edge of the university campus. Where he remembered vast oak hummocks, there were rectilinear brick buildings. Mossy pools were now parking lots.

Only his father's property, one hundred acres, was overgrown with palmettos and vines. He brushed the red bugs off his wife's sensible travel pants and carried her into his father's house. Termites had chiseled long gouges in the floorboards, but the sturdy Cracker house had kept out most of the wilderness. His wife touched the mantel made of heart pine and turned to him gladly. Later, after he came home with a box of groceries and found the kitchen scrubbed clean, he heard three thumps upstairs and ran up to find that she had killed a black snake in the bathtub with her bare heel and was laughing at herself in amazement.

How magnificent he found her, a Valkyrie, half naked and warlike with that dead snake at her feet. In her body, the culmination of all things. He didn't say it, of course; he couldn't. He only reached and put his hands upon her.

In the night, she rolled toward him and took his ankles between her own. All right, she said. We can stay.

I didn't say anything, he said.

And she smiled a little bitterly and said, Well. You don't.

They moved their things into the house where he was born. They put in air-conditioning, renovated the structure, put on large additions. His wife opened a shop and drove to Miami and Atlanta to stock it with antiques. He sold his father's land, but slowly, in small pieces, at prices that rose dizzyingly with each sale. The numbers lived in him, warmed him, brought him a buzzing kind of joy. Jude made investments so shrewd that when he and his wife were in their mid-thirties, he opened a bottle of wine and announced that neither of them would ever have to work again. His wife laughed and drank but kept up with the store.

When she was almost too old, they had a daughter and named her after his mother.

When he held the baby at home for the first time, he understood he had never been so terrified of anything as he was of this mottled lump of flesh. How easily he could break her without meaning to. She could slip from his hands and crack open on the floor; she could catch pneumonia when he bathed her; he could say a terrible thing in anger and she would shrivel. All the mistakes he could make telescoped before him. His wife saw him turn pale and plucked the baby from his hands just before he crashed down. When he came to, she was livid but calm. He protested, but she put the baby in his hands.

Try again, she said.

His daughter grew, sturdy and blonde like his wife, with no ash of Jude's genius for numbers. They were as dry as biscuits in her mouth; she preferred music and English. For this, he was glad. She would love more moderately, more externally. If he didn't cuddle with her the way her mother did, he still thought he was a good father: he never hit her, he never left her alone in the house, he told her how much he loved her by providing her with everything he could imagine she'd like. He was a quiet parent, but he was sure she knew the scope of his heart.

And yet his daughter never grew out of wearing a singularly irritating expression, one taut with competition, which she first wore when she was a very little girl at an Easter egg hunt. She could barely walk in her grass-stained bloomers, but even when the other children rested out of the Florida sunshine in the shade, eating their booty of chocolate, Jude's little girl kept returning with eggs too cunningly hidden in the sago palms to have been found in the first frenzy. She heaped them on his lap until they overflowed, and she shrieked when he told her firmly that enough was enough.

～

His fat old uncle came over for dinner once, then once a week, then became a friend. When the uncle died of an aneurysm while feeding his canary, he left Jude his estate of moth-eaten smoking jackets and family photos in ornate frames.

The university grew around Jude's last ten-acre parcel, a protective cushion between the old house and the rest of the world. The more construction around their plot of land, the fewer snakes Jude saw, until he felt no qualms about walking barefoot in the St. Augustine grass to take the garbage to the edge of the drive. He built a fence around his land and laughed at the university's offers, sensing desperation in their inflating numbers. He thought of himself as the virus in the busy cell, latent, patient. The swamp's streams were blocked by the university's construction, and it became a small lake, in which he installed some bubblers to keep the mosquitoes away. There were alligators, sometimes large ones, but he put in an invisible fence, and it kept his family's dogs from coming too close to the water's edge and being gobbled up. The gators only eyed them from the banks.

And then, one day, Jude woke with the feeling that a bell jar had descended over him. He showered with a sense of unease, sat at the edge of the bed for a while. When his wife came in to tell him something, he watched in confusion at the way her mouth opened and closed fishily, without sound.

I think I've gone deaf, he said, and he didn't so much hear his words as feel them vibrating in the bones of his skull.

At the doctor's, he submitted to test after test, but nobody understood what had gone wrong in his brain or in his ears. They gave him a hearing aid that turned conversation into an underwater burble. Mostly, he kept it off.

At night, he'd come out into the dark kitchen, longing for curried chicken, raw onion, preserved peaches, tastes sharp and simple to remind himself that he was still there. He'd find his daughter at the kitchen island, her lovely mean face lit up by her screen. She'd frown at him and turn the screen to show him what she'd discovered: cochlear implants, audiologic rehabilitation, miracles.

But there was nothing for him. He was condemned. He ate Thanksgiving dinner wanting to weep into his sweet potatoes. His family was gathered around him, his wife and daughter and their closest friends and their children, and he could see them laughing, but he couldn't hear the jokes. He longed for someone to look up, to see him at the end of the table, to reach out a hand and pat his. But they were too happy. They slotted full forks into their mouths and brought the tines out clean. They picked the flesh off the turkey, they scooped the pecans out of the pie.

After the dinner, his arms prickling with hot water from the dishes, they sat together watching football, and he lay back in his chair with his feet propped up, and all of the children fell asleep around him on the couch, and he alone sat in vigil over them, watching them sleep.

～

The day his daughter went to college in Boston, his wife went with her.

She mouthed very carefully to him, You'll be all right for four days? You can take care of yourself?

And he said, Yes, of course. I am an *adult*, sweetheart, but the way she winced, he knew he'd said it too loudly. He loaded their bags into the car, and his daughter cried in his arms, and he kissed her over and over on the crown of the head. His wife looked at him worriedly but kissed him also and climbed inside. And then, silently as everything, the car moved off.

The house felt immense around him. He sat in the study, which had been his childhood bedroom, and seemed to see the place as it had been, spare and filled with snakes, layered atop the house as it was, with its marble and bright walls and track lights above his head.

That night, he waited, his hearing aid turned up so loudly that it began to make sharp beeping sounds that hurt. He wanted the pain. He fell asleep watching a sitcom that, without sound, was just strange-looking people making huge expressions with their faces, and he woke up and it was only eight o'clock at night, and he felt as if he'd been alone forever.

He hadn't known he'd miss his wife's heavy body in the bed next to his, the sandwiches she made (too much mayonnaise, but he never told her so), the smell of her bodywash in the humid bathroom in the morning.

On the second night, he sat in the black density of the veranda, looking at the lake that used to be a swamp. He wondered what had happened to the reptiles out there, where they had gone. Alone in the darkness, Jude wished he could hear the university in its nighttime boil around him, the students shouting drunkenly, the bass thrumming, the noise of football games out at the stadium that used to make Jude and his wife groan with irritation. But he could have been anywhere, in the middle of hundreds of miles of wasteland, as quiet as the night was for him. Even the mosquitoes had somehow diminished. As a child, he would have been a single itchy blister by now.

Unable to sleep, Jude climbed to the roof to straighten the gutter that had crimped in the middle from a falling oak branch. He crept on his hands and knees across the asbestos shingles, still hot from the day, to fix the flashing on the chimney. From up there, the university coiled around him, and in the streetlights, a file of pledging sorority girls in tight, bright dresses and high heels slowly crawled up the hill like ants.

He came down reluctantly at dawn and took a can of tuna and a cold jug of water down to the lake's edge, where he turned over the aluminum johnboat his wife had bought for him a few years earlier, hoping he'd take up fishing.

Fishing? he'd said, I haven't fished since I was a boy. He thought of those childhood shad and gar and snook, how his father cooked them up with the lemons from the tree beside the back door and ate them without a word of praise. He must have made a face because his wife had recoiled.

I thought it'd be a hobby, she'd said. If you don't like it, find another hobby. Or *something*.

He'd thanked her but had never had the time to use either the rod or the boat. It sat there, its bright belly dulling under layers of pollen. Now was the time. He was hungry for something indefinable, something he thought he'd left behind him so long ago. He thought he might find it in the lake, perhaps.

He pushed off and rowed out. There was no wind, and the sun was already searing. The water was hot and thick with algae. A heron stood one-legged among the cypress. Something big jumped and sent rings out toward the boat, rocking it slightly. Jude tried to get comfortable but was sweating, and now the mosquitoes smelled him and swarmed. The silence was eerie because he remembered the lake as a dense tapestry of sound, the click and whirr of the sandhill cranes, the cicadas, the owls, the mysterious subhuman cries too distant to identify. He had wanted to connect with something, something he had lost, but it wasn't here.

He gave up. But when he sat up to row himself back, both oars had slid loose from their locks and floated off. They lay ten feet away, caught in the duckweed.

The water thickly hid its danger, but he knew what was there. There were the alligators, their knobby eyes even now watching him. He'd seen one with his binoculars from the bedroom the other day that was at least fourteen feet long. He felt it somewhere nearby now. And though this was no longer prairie, there were still a few snakes, cottonmouths, copperheads, pygmies under the leaf rot at the edge of the lake. There was the water itself, superheated until it hosted flagellates that enter the nose and infect the brain, an infinity of the minuscule eating away. There was the burning sun above and the mosquitoes feeding on his blood. There was the silence. He wouldn't swim in this terrifying mess. He stood, agitated, and felt the boat slide a few inches from under him, and he sat down hard, clinging to the gunwales. He was a hundred feet offshore on a breathless day. He would not be blown to shore. He would be stuck here forever; his wife would come home in two days to find his corpse floating in its johnboat. He drank some water to calm himself. When he decided to remember algorithms in his head, their savor had stolen away.

For now, there were silent birds and sun and mosquitoes; below, a world of slinking predators. In the delicate cup of the johnboat, he was alone. He closed his eyes and felt his heart beat in his ears.

He had never had the time to be seized by doubt. Now all he had was time. Hours dripped past. He sweated. He was ill. The sun only grew hotter, and there was no respite, no shade.

Jude drifted off to sleep, and when he woke, he knew that if he opened his eyes, he would see his father sitting in the bow, glowering. Terrible son, Jude was, to ruin what his father loved best. The ancient fear rose in him, and he swallowed it as well as he could with his dry throat. He would not open his eyes, he wouldn't give the old man the satisfaction.

Go away, he said. Leave me be. His voice inside his head was only a rumble.

His father waited, patient and silent, a dark dense mass at the end of the boat.

I'm not like you, Dad, Jude said later. I don't prefer snakes to people.

The sun pushed down; the smell on the air was his father's smell. Jude breathed from his mouth.

Even later, he said, You were a nasty, unhappy man.

And I always hated you.

But this seemed harsh, and he said, I didn't completely mean that.

He thought of this lake. He thought of how his father would see Jude's life. Such a delicate ecosystem, so precisely calibrated, in the end destroyed by Jude's careful parceling of love, of land. Greed, the university's gobble. Those scaled creatures, killed. The awe in his father's voice that day they went out gathering moccasins; the bright, sharp love inside Jude, long ago, when he had loved numbers. Jude's promise was unfulfilled, the choices made not the passionate ones. Jude had been safe.

And still, here he was. Alone as his father was when he died in that tent. Isolated. Sunbattered. Old.

He thought in despair of diving into the perilous water, and how he probably deserved being bitten. But then the wind picked up and began pushing him back across the lake, toward his house. When he opened his eyes, his father wasn't with him, but the house loomed over the bow, ramshackle, too huge, a crazy person's place. He averted his eyes, unable to bear it now. The sun snuffed itself out. Despite his pain, the skin on his legs and arms blistered with sunburn and great, itching mosquito welts, he later realized he must have fallen asleep because, when he opened his eyes again, the stars were out and the johnboat was nosing up against the shore.

He stood, his bones aching, and wobbled to the shore.

And now something white and large was rushing at him, and because he'd sat all day with his father's ghost, he understood this was a ghost, too, and looked up at it, calm and ready. The lights from the house shined at its back, and it had a golden glow around it. But the figure stopped just before him, and he saw, with a startle, that it was his wife, that the glow was her frizzy gray hair catching the light, and he knew then that she must have come back early, that she was reaching a hand out to him, putting her soft palm on his cheek, and she was saying something forever lost to him, but he knew by the way she was smiling that she was scolding him. He stepped closer to her and put his head in the crook of her neck and breathed his inadequacy out there, breathed in her love and the grease of her travels and knew he had been lucky, and that he had escaped the hungry dark once more.

THE HAPPY PLACE

JOYCE CAROL OATES

Professor! Hello.

White winter days, sunshine on newly fallen snow. You have come to the *happy place* for it is Thursday afternoon.

Another week, and you are still alive. Your secret you carry everywhere and so into the *happy place.*

So close to the heart, no one will see.

~

Not a happy season. Not a happy time. Not in the history of the world and not in the personal lives of many.

You wonder how many are like you. Having come to prefer dark to daylight. Sweet oblivion of sleep to raw wakefulness.

Yet: in the wood-paneled seminar room on the fifth floor of North Hall. At the top of the smooth-worn wooden staircase where a leaded window overlooks a stand of juniper pines. In the wind, pine boughs shiver and flash with melting snow. The *happy place.*

Here is an atmosphere of optimism light as helium. You laugh often, you and the undergraduates spaced about the polished table.

Why do you laugh so much?—you have wondered.

Generally it seems: the more serious the subjects, the more likely some sort of laughter.

The more intensity, the more laughter.

The more at stake, the more laughter.

The *happy place* is the solace. The promise.

Waking in the morning stunned to be *still alive.* The profound fact of your life now.

~

Already at the first class meeting in September you'd noticed her: *Ana.*

Of the twelve students in the fiction writing workshop it is *Ana* who holds herself apart from the others. From you.

When they laugh, Ana does not laugh—not often.

When they answer questions you put to them, when in their enthusiasm they talk over one another like puppies tumbling together—Ana sits silent. Though Ana may look on with a faint (melancholy) smile.

Or, Ana may turn her gaze toward the wall of windows casting a ghostly reflected light onto her face and seem to be staring into space—oblivious of her surroundings.

Thinking her own thoughts. Private, not yours to know.

You feel an impulse to lean across the table, to touch Ana's wrist. To smile at her, ask—*Ana, is something wrong?*

But what would you dare ask this girl who holds herself apart from her classmates? *Are you troubled? Unhappy? Distracted? Bored?*—not possible. One of the others in the seminar might take Ana aside to ask such questions but you, the adult in the room, the Professor, don't have that right, nor would you exercise that right if indeed it were yours. Still less should you touch Ana's wrist.

It is a very thin wrist. The wrist of a child. So easily snapped! The young woman's face is delicately boned, pale, smooth as porcelain, her eyes are beautiful and thick-lashed but somewhat shadowed, evasive.

You have noticed, around Ana's slender neck, a thin gold chain with a small gold cross.

The little cross must be positioned just so, in the hollow at the base of Ana's throat, that is as pronounced and (once you have noticed it) conspicuous as your own.

(What is it called?—*suprasternal notch.* A physical feature aligned with thinness, generally conceded to be a genetic inheritance.)

Indeed, Ana is a very diminutive young woman. To the casual eye she would seem more likely fourteen than eighteen and hardly a *woman* at all.

Ana must weigh less than one hundred pounds. No more than five feet two. You see, without having actually noticed until now, that she wears loose-fitting clothing, a shapeless pullover several sizes too large, and the thought strikes you, unbidden, fleeting, that Ana may be acutely *thin*. Her diffident manner makes her appear even smaller. *As if she might curl up, disappear. Cast no shadow.*

How vulnerable Ana appears!—to gaze upon her is to feel that you must protect her.

Yet, you suppose that there are many who would wish to take advantage of her.

When the others speak of "religious belief"—"superstition"—with the heedlessness of bright adolescents wielding their wits like blades Ana sits very still at her end of the table, eyes downcast. Touching the cross around her neck.

Why doesn't Ana speak, intervene? Defend her beliefs, if indeed she has beliefs?

Yes. This is a superstitious symbol I am wearing. What is it to you?

The discussion has risen out of the week's assignment, a short story by Flannery O'Connor saturated with Christian imagery and the mystery of the Eucharist, and Ana, like the others, has written an analysis of the story.

But Ana remains silent, stiff until at last the discussion veers in another direction. Glancing at you, an expression of—is it reproach? hurt?—for just an instant.

∼

The *insomniac night* is the antithesis of the *happy place*.

Unlike the *happy place* which is specifically set, and unfortunately finite, as an academic class invariably comes to an end, the *insomniac night* has no natural end.

If you cannot sleep in the night, the night will simply continue into the next, sun-blinding day.

∼

You have thought *Is she a refugee* for her spoken English is hesitant, imperfect. You have not wanted to think *Is she a victim. Has she been hurt. What is the sorrow in her face. Why is she so unlike the others.*

Ana's face, that seems wise beyond her years. (You are certain you are not misinterpreting.)

Oh, why does Ana not *smile?* Why is it Ana who alone resists the *happy place?*

In twenty-seven years of teaching you have encountered a number of *Ana's*—surely.

Yet, you don't recall. Not one. And why should you, students are impermanent in the lives of teachers. There is nothing profound in this situation. Ana has done adequate work for the course, she has never failed to hand in her work on time. You have no reason to ask her to come and speak with you, no reason at all.

Ana's reluctance (refusal?) to smile on cue, as others so easily smile— this is a small mystery.

Is it your pride that is hurt? But how little pride means to you, frankly.

You are conscious of the (unwitting) tyranny of the group. Of any group no matter how congenial, well-intentioned.

That all in the group laugh, smile, agree with the others, or "disagree" politely, or flirtatiously. The (unwitting) tyranny of the classroom that even the most liberal-minded instructor cannot fail to exert. *Pay attention to me. Pay attention to the forward-motion of the class. No silences! No inward-turning—this is not a Zen meditation. A small class is a sort of skiff, we are all paddling. We are all responsible for paddling. We are aiming for the same destination. We are aware (some of us keenly) of those who are not paddling. Those who have set their paddles aside.*

Perhaps Ana has not clearly understood that enrollment in a small seminar brings with it a degree of responsibility for participation. Answering questions, asking questions. "Discussing." The workshop is not a lecture course: students are not expected to take notes. Perhaps it was an error in judgment for Ana to enroll in a course in which (it seems apparent) she has so little interest as, you are thinking, it was an error in judgment for you to accept her application, out of seventy applications for a workshop of twelve.

Why had you chosen Ana Fallas? A first-year student, with no background in creative writing? Something in the writing sample Ana had provided must have appealed to you, a glimpse of Hispanic domestic life perhaps, that set it aside from others that were merely good, conventional.

Though now, as it has turned out, Ana's work has seemed less exceptional. Careful, circumspect. Nothing grammatically wrong but—nothing to call attention to itself.

As if Ana is trying to make herself into one of *them*—the Caucasian majority.

It is likely that Ana is intimidated by the university—its size, its reputation. By the other students in the writing class. She is but one of only two first-year students, and the other is Shan from Beijing, a dazzling prodigy intending to major in neuroscience.

The others are older than Ana, more experienced. Three are seniors, immersed in original research—senior theses. Most of them are Americans and those who are not, like Shan, and Ansar (Pakistan), and Colin (UK), have studied in the United States previously and seem to have traveled widely. Ana is the only Hispanic student in the class and (you are guessing) she might be the first in her family to have enrolled in college.

Is Ana aware of you, your concern for her? Sometimes you think *yes*. More often you think *no. Not at all.*

⁓

I can't.

Or, *I don't think that I can…*

At the age of twenty-two you were terrified at the prospect of teaching your first class.

English Composition. A large urban university. An evening class.

More than a quarter-century ago and yet—vivid in memory!

You had never taught before. You had a master's degree in English but had never been (like most of your graduate student friends, and your husband) a teaching assistant. Amazing to you now, that the chairman of an English Department in a quite reputable private university had hired you to teach though you'd had no experience teaching at all—had not once stood in front of a classroom. (He'd said afterward that he had been impressed by the written work of yours he'd seen, in national publications. He'd said that, in his experience, teaching was best picked up *on the fly*, like learning to ride a bicycle, or like sex.)

It had been thrilling to you, to be so selected over numerous others with experience, older than you. But it had not been so thrilling to contemplate the actual teaching. At twenty-two you would not be much older, in fact you would be younger, than many of your students enrolled in the university's night school division.

English composition! The most commonly taught of university courses, along with remedial English and math.

Your husband, young himself at the time, just thirty, had tried to dispel your terror. He'd tried to encourage you, tease you. Saying—*Don't be afraid, I can walk you into the classroom on my shoes.*

Such a silly notion, you'd laughed. Tears of apprehension in your eyes and yet you'd laughed, your husband had that power, to calm you.

Between your young husband and you, in those years. Much laughter.

You think you will live forever. Always it will be like this. You don't think—well, you don't think.

Your husband had a PhD in English. He was an assistant professor at another, nearby university, he'd been a very successful teacher for several years. Gently he reasoned with you: what could possibly go wrong, once you'd prepared for the first class?

What could go wrong? Everything!

They won't pay attention to me. They will see that I am too young—inexperienced. They will laugh in derision. Some of them will walk out...

Your husband convinced you that such fears were groundless. Ridiculous. University students would not walk out of a class. Especially older students would not walk out of a class for which they'd paid tuition—it was a serious business to them, not a lark.

In this class, so long ago, were thirty students. Thirty! Over-large for a composition class.

To you, thirty strangers. You broke into actual sweat, contemplating them. The prospect of entering the classroom was dazzling. A nightmare.

For days beforehand you rehearsed your first words—*Hello! This is English one-oh-one and my name is*—which you hoped would not be stammered, and would be audible. For days you pondered—what should you *wear?*

On that crucial evening your husband drove you to the university. Your husband did not *walk you into the room on his shoes* but he did accompany you to the assigned classroom in the ground floor of an old red-brick building. (Did your husband kiss you, for good luck? A brush of his lips on your cheek?) How breathless you were by this time, seeing your prospective students pass you oblivious of you.

Wish me luck.

I love you!

And so it happened when you stepped into the classroom, and took your place behind a podium in front of a blackboard, and introduced yourself to rows of strangers gazing at you with the most rapt interest you'd ever drawn from any strangers in your life—an unexpected and astonishing conviction flooded over you of *happiness.*

Knowing you were in the right place, at just the right time.

~

You feel her absence keenly.

This day, a particularly wet, cold day Ana is absent from the workshop.

Reluctant to begin class you wait for several minutes. (For other students are arriving late.) Then, when it is evident that Ana will not be coming, you begin.

You have noticed that Ana sits in the same place at the table each week. She will arrive early, to assure this. Such (rigid?) behavior is the sign of a shy person; a person who has had enough upset in her life, and now wants a predictable routine; a person who chooses to rein in her emotions; a person who knows that, like internal hemorrhaging, emotions are not infinite, and can be fatal.

Tacitly the others have conceded Ana's place at the (farther) end of the table. No one would take Ana's chair, just as no one would take the Professor's usual seat.

Yet, no one mentions Ana's absence. So little impression has she made on the class, no one thinks to wonder aloud—*Hey, where is Ana?*

You ask for a volunteer, to provide Ana with the assignment for the following week. At first no one responds. Then a young woman raises her hand—*Sure! She's in my residence hall, I think.*

You might email or text Ana yourself. But you are thinking you would like someone from the workshop to volunteer, to forge a connection with Ana however slight.

~

That evening Ana sends you an email, apologizing for her absence. *Flu, infirmary sorry to miss class. Will make up missing work.*

~

Ridiculous, you are *so relieved.*

Smiling, your heart suffused with—what? Hope like a helium-filled balloon.

When Ana returns to the workshop you tell her—*We missed you, Ana.*

True, to a degree. *You* missed her.

Naturally Ana has completed the assignment: the reading in the anthology, and the weekly prose piece. Though Ana is not one of the more imaginative writers, Ana is the most diligent of students.

Hers has been good work, acceptable work so far this semester. It is careful work, precisely written English, surprisingly free of errors for one whose speech is uncertain. Is this the utterance of clenched jaws?—you wonder. Maybe Ana would like to scream.

You will encourage her to write more freely. From the heart.

You will tell her—in fact, you will tell the class—*Write what feels like life to you. It need not be "true"—your writing will make it "true."*

Ana frowns distractedly, staring down at the table. She knows that you are (obliquely) criticizing her work, which the others have discussed politely, without much to say about it. For all her pose of indifference Ana is highly sensitive.

You have encouraged your students to write, not memoir, but *memoir-like* fiction. You do not (truly!) want these young people to open their veins and pour out their life's blood for the diversion of others but neither do you want them to attempt arch, artificial fiction derivative of work by the most-read fiction writers of the era—for that they cannot do, and certainly they cannot do well.

Others in the class take up the challenge, excited. *Write what feels like life to you.*

Ana takes back her prose piece from you. Ana's eyes slide away from yours and will not engage.

You had written—*Promising! But something that anyone might have written. What does "Ana" have to say?*

Away from the seminar room which is the *happy place* you ponder your obsession with this student. For the first time acknowledging the word—*obsession.*

Telling yourself that now you've made the acknowledgment, the *obsession* will begin to fade.

∼

And then, in the seventh week of the semester, long past the time when you'd have thought that any undergraduate could surprise you, Ana hands in something very different from the cautious prose she has been writing.

The assignment is a dramatic monologue. Just a page or two. In the "memoirist" mode.

Here is urgent, intense work by Ana. Not cautious at all—a bold plunge into stream-of-consciousness speech uttered (seemingly) by an adolescent daughter of (Guatemalan?) (illegal?) immigrants stranded in a nightmare detention center at the Texas border in Laredo.

The other young writers take notice. It is requested that Ana read the monologue aloud.

Oh, I—I can't....

Stammering *no*, blushing fiercely but the others insist.

∼

From a prose poem of Ana's: *I thought the eucalyptus had burst into flame, I'd seen it and ran away screaming. And then—years later they laugh at me and told me no, that had not happened to me but to my little sister.*

And when I remember my brother beaten by our father with his fists they tell me no, not just my brother but me, as well. But they are not laughing.

In the foster home there are three girls named Mya.

Those acts perpetrated upon one of the Myas are perpetrated upon the others.

We do not know your name but your face will always be known to us.

∼

Astonishing and wonderful—Ana is writing with such passion now.

Less guardedly, and less circumspectly. Wonderful too, how others in the seminar take up her work with excitement and admiration.

This is not conventional "fiction"—there are few "characters"—minimal "description"—"settings." All is dreamlike, rapid-fire.

In fragments it is revealed that a girl named "Mya" has lived in one or more foster homes in the Southwest. Albuquerque, Tucson. In the home are (illegal?) Central American immigrants. There are bribes to be paid. There are hopes for visas, green cards. There are knives, guns. Brutal beatings when debts are not repaid. Shootings, woundings, blood-soaked mattresses. A ghastly scene in an emergency room where an eighteen-year-old Guatemalan hemorrhages to death, and a laconic scene in a morgue in which a drug-addled woman attempts to identify an estranged and badly mutilated husband. Hiding from law enforcement officers, rummaging Dumpsters for food. Shoplifting. Unexpected cruelty in the foster home, and unexpected kindness.

Homeless children, adolescents. A girl seeking out a younger sister who has been sent to live in a foster home.

There was no choice. My mother believed our father would kill her if she did not leave.

...first there were three Myas in the foster home. Then there were two Myas. Then there was one Mya.

Then, none.

~

You are filled with dread, you have gone too far. Your shy, unassertive student has begun writing *what feels like life*—she has thrown off restraint.

It is true, you have triumphed—as a writing instructor. But this is a precarious triumph—(maybe). As if you have prized open a shell, the pulsing life of the defenseless mollusk within is exposed.

One of the most imaginative writers in the class, whose name is Philip, whose major is astrophysics and whose favored writers are Borges, Calvino, Cortazar, declares that Ana's prose poetry is *beautiful and terrible as a Mobius strip.*

Ana is deeply moved to hear these words. You have seen how Philip has been casting sidelong glances at Ana, over the weeks; now Ana lifts her eyes to his face.

Much attention is paid in the workshop to Ana's prose. Her sentences, paragraphs—headlong plunges of language. There is praise for Ana's spare, elliptical dialogue which is buried in the text as if it might be interior and not uttered aloud at all.

No one cares to address Ana's powerful subject matter. Desperate persons, domestic violence, a hint of sexual assault. *Three girls named Mya in the foster home.*

Amid their admiration the others are uneasy. It is considered bad manners—the violation of an implicit taboo—to ask if anyone's work is based upon her experiences, at least when the work is so extreme. And you have taken care to instruct the students, memoirist writing is *not memoir.* Even memoir is not "autobiography" but understood to be more poetic and impressionistic, less literal and complete.

At the end of the discussion Ana is flushed with pleasure. Unless it's an excited sort of dread. Never have you seen Ana so intense, so involved in the workshop.

You would not dare reach out to touch her wrist now, her burning-hot skin would scald your fingers.

～

The following Thursday Ana is not in the seminar room when you arrive.

Everyone waits for Ana's arrival. The chair in which she usually sits is left unoccupied. But she does not appear.

Your heart is seized with dismay. You are sure it's as you'd feared—Ana regrets what she revealed to the class, she regrets being led to such openness.

Having written what she has written, that cannot now be retracted.

I am so sorry, Ana. Forgive me.

You don't write such an email. Never!

From your husband you learned never to impose your emotions upon students. Never to assume to know what they are thinking and feeling, that is (but) what you imagine they are thinking and feeling, unless they tell you; and it would be rare indeed for them to tell you.

You are the adult. You are the professional. You must prevail.

～

And then: by chance you encounter Ana in a store near the university. Indeed it is but *by chance*. Indeed *you have not been following Ana.*

Seeing too, another time—how alone Ana appears. How small, vulnerable.

Inside an oversized winter coat falling nearly to her ankles, that looks like a hand-me-down.

Her face is flushed from the cold, her eyes startled and damp. Faint shadows like bruises in her perfect skin, beneath her eyes.

Though you can see that Ana would (probably) prefer not to say hello it is not possible for you to avoid each other. You greet Ana with a friendly smile as you would any student, ignoring her nervousness; she stammers *Hello Professor...*

Ana is embarrassed, awkward. Still, Ana manages to smile at her professor.

Telling you apologetically that she'd meant to write to you, to explain why she'd had to miss another class: there'd been a family emergency, she'd had to spend time on the phone with several relatives. Ana speaks so rapidly, in faltering English, you halfway wonder if she is telling the truth. Yet in her face an expression of such genuine dismay you are sure that she must be telling some part of the truth.

You are thinking *If this were a story...*you would invite Ana to have coffee with you, perhaps you would walk together in the lightly falling snow, and talk. Ana would confide in you at last, directly; as, it has seemed to you, she is confiding in you indirectly, in her writing. Ana would reveal herself the survivor of abuse, a broken and devastated household. A traumatized child in need of advice, protection...

But that does not happen. Will not happen. For this is not a story, and not a fiction. This is actual life, that does not bend easily to your fantasies.

The moment passes. You move on. You do not glance after Ana, as, you are sure, Ana does not glance after you.

It is true, you are desperately lonely. But you understand that yours is an adult loneliness that no adolescent stranger can assuage.

$\sim$

Recalling your shock, and subsequently melancholy, when the first class of your life came to an end.

How you'd actually wept...*I will never have such wonderful students again.*
Your husband comforted you though (surely) he'd been amused.
Twenty-seven years ago.

~

As abruptly as it seemed to have begun, the semester has ended.

The final workshop in the wood-paneled seminar room at the top of the smooth-worn staircase in North Hall.

And then, reading week—between the end of classes and the start of exams. You will see students through this week, you have made appointments with each of the writers in the workshop. Following these conferences it's likely that you will not see most of the students again.

After such intimacy, abrupt detachment. The way of teaching—semester following semester.

Professor! Hello...

There is Ana, in the doorway of your office. Accompanied by two tensely smiling adults—parents?

You don't expect this. You are totally surprised. You'd thought—what had you thought?

A lost girl, an abused girl. An orphan.

Though Ana appears to be virtually quivering with nerves, or with excitement, she has brought her parents to meet you—*Elena and Carlos Fallas.* Ana's pride in the situation, her thrilled face, shining eyes, the way she clasps her parents' hands in hers, urging them to enter your office—it is very touching, you are moved nearly to tears.

Ana's parents are so *young.* Especially the mother who is Ana's height, small-boned, with beautiful dark eyes. Haltingly the parents speak to you in heavily accented English. They are visiting from San Diego, they say. They have heard much about *you.*

Through a roaring in your ears you hear Ana speaking of her favorite class, her writing class, how you helped her to write *as if your life depended upon it.*

How you'd told her—*It need not be true, your writing will make it true.*

Ana is breathless, daring. What an achievement it has been for your shyest student to have brought her parents to meet you! How long has Ana been practicing these words, this encounter...

The scene seems impossible to you. Unreal. How had you so misread Ana Fallas? Her seeming lack of interest in the seminar, and in you... Her sorrowful expression, her isolation...

Had you misinterpreted, and Ana is not telling the fullest truth now? But rather, performing for her parents? And for you?

The melancholy was not feigned, you are sure. The sorrow in her eyes. Yet—here is a very different Ana, laughing as she discreetly corrects her parents' English, vivacious and sparkling, happy.

Ana has plaited her hair into a sleekly black braid. She has painted her fingernails coral. She is wearing, not baggy clothes, but attractive bright-colored clothing that is a perfect size for her small body. The little gold cross glitters around her neck. Ana is very pretty, and she is adored by her parents. She is not an abused child, she is certainly not an orphan.

Astonishingly, you hear—*My favorite professor.*

You are determined not to betray this astonishment. You are determined to speak despite the roaring in your ears. Assuring Ana's eager parents that Ana has been an excellent student. A very promising writer. Like few young writers, Ana can learn from criticism—constructive criticism. Ana's imagination is fertile, seemingly boundless. You are giddy as a drunkard. Words tumble from your mouth, you are shameless. You will say anything to please these people, you want only to make them happy, to make them less ill-at-ease in your professorial presence.

You will not confess—*I have been so mistaken about your daughter. I am ashamed...*

She is not the person I had imagined. You are not the people. Forgive me!

Ana's parents have brought you a beautifully wrapped little gift. Your heart sinks, you hope it isn't expensive. (That size? Could be a small clock. A watch.) You have not the heart to decline their generosity but it is considered a breech of academic ethics, at least at this university, to accept gifts from the parents of students, even small gifts.

The card from Ana you will accept, with thanks. The gift you will pass to the departmental secretary.

Ana's parents are less nervous now. They tell you how proud they are of their daughter, the first in the family to attend a four-year college.

How grateful for the scholarship that brought her here—though it is so far from home. How honored to meet you.

When they leave you stand in the doorway of your office staring after them, still disbelieving, dazed. *So mistaken. How possible...*

The little gift you leave on your desk for the time being. The card from Ana you open: *Thank you, Professor, for giving me the key to my life.*

~

And then, returning home later that evening.

A mild shock—the door is unlocked.

Turn the knob, and the door opens. Not for the first time since your husband has died. It is a careless habit, away for hours and the house unlocked and darkened.

You have become careless with your life. Indifferent.

Entering an empty house from which all meaning has fled.

Once, this was a *happy place.* That seems like a bad joke now.

Each room in this house is a kind of exile. You avoid most of the rooms, you keep in motion. Difficult to find a place to sit, a place where you are comfortable sitting. Almost at once you feel restless, anxious. Your fingers clutch at the hollow in your throat, you have difficulty breathing.

He has been gone how many months. Still you cannot—quite—acknowledge the word *dead.*

Once, you'd known precisely how many weeks, days. Down to the hour.

But the house is still as deserted. This place from which happiness has drained like water seeping into earth.

You have tried to explain to your husband, as you try to explain to him so many things, for he is patient, unjudging—how you were mistaken about Ana, for so long. The stubbornness in your misperception, the *hurt.* You have tried, and failed, to explain to him why Ana has meant so much to you. And why it has all ended, as it has ended.

It is frightening to you, in this empty and darkened house—*What else has eluded you, that is staring you in the face? About what else have you been mistaken?*

FOUR POEMS

JESSICA LASER
SIMPSON FELLOW

TASTE

All my life I've asked my master
Why I am unable to choose
This sweet man or fancy shoes
Over this stranger, more difficult lover
And these expensive but practical loafers

And why I am unable to author
A book exhibiting my full potential
And have focused instead on inconsequential
Letters to strange and difficult lovers
Who by my letters were never changed.

I certainly haven't been constrained
By terrible parents or trauma or poverty
And even if I had it wouldn't explain
My propensity for misery
Anymore than it would my
Propensity for joy.

Maybe I'm just a procrastinator
As life is a procrastination of death
And each breath just a procrastination of breath
And friends a procrastination of work
And work a procrastination of love
And love a procrastination I'm just not above.

THE ROCK

I tried to chase the phantom.
I stood in it. I recognized a deficit
The problem located
In me or others
But in that the phantom
Could not be addressed
I reached out and it
Addressed itself to me.
Life is a process
A pretty glow from a lamp
A cloud glowers over
And troubles the phantom
Within that assumption.
So me I couldn't say what I received.
I was relieved. That was the phantom
And I the recipient
Could not be addressed but to it.

SENSUAL DELIGHT IN VIRTUE

Ciao ciao ciao ciao
Bella bella bella bella

I don't exist to appear
I exist to exist

This mass couldn't be anymore
On the radio

She is overlooking me
She is, it's true

She's looking for something that doesn't appear
She will one day make it visible

I don't exist to appear
I exist to exist

And I went there, too.

When a fly hurts, it scans
Where it might have flown
With weird optical versions
Of longing. Your body hurts
And hurts. When your mind
Hurts, it has thoughts
That hurt you. For example,
How could I divorce
Someone to whom I'm
Unwilling to pay alimony?
And I went there, too

Because I understanded.
I completed a family
Met along the river
As it levels out.

It was in this very depression
Between two hills
That I rode.

When I complete a family
We are never better, never
Than when our enemies love us
Which is to say when we fail.
But Sergei Kuzmich from all sides
There is no treason to describe.

When a fly hurts, it scans.
When your body hurts
It hurts. When your mind
Hurts, its thoughts
Hurt you. For example,
How could I divorce
Someone to whom I
Went there, too
Because I understanded,
I completed a family
Met along the river
As it levels out.

It was this very depression
Between two hills
That I straddled.

Gentlemen, I said as you were!
But she is overlooking me!
So she is! It's true! She's looking for something that doesn't appear
But one day she will make it visible
For though those arms are leprous as snow, it takes soft arms

To tear down fences, soft features
To exist to appear.

I exist to exist.
When I complete a family
We are never better, never
And our enemies love us.

AGAINST DOOM

If you could capture doom and make it
beautiful, you'd make it icy like a sea.
You'd make the sky look up to it,
the rest of a wave under which we live.

At times there'd be no
sky at all, only sky
we wade in when we feel
we're what we see.

Doom is a planet, the views, the overhanging
vines and I live in a time of fruition,
obsessed with fun, feeling myself part of it,
a relic, a ruined thing.

The sky and sea are breaking.
The sun sets at a pace of ice
the ice itself is barred from.
Imagine you unite with what you see,

pain in a child, and that every unity
brings divisions as you cleave
from what you see ahead to meet it,
the child in pain.

The pace of the wave
we live under the crest of
the mind itself sets like a sea.
I try to unite my mind with me.

It rises like a setting,
a planet circling the nearest sun,
each sun a throat with hands around it,
this pain has nothing to do with me.

TWO POEMS

LISE GASTON
SIMPSON FELLOW

STEP: AN ANATOMY OF THE FOOT

talus

it helps us simulate balance
as the small boat rocks, horizon

steady while vision tilts, we dance
to the heave and a rockfish crescents

the line, arches its poisonous
back, gasping, our collective hands

twist the red fish from its hook, all
head, we toss it unblinking to

the surface where it stays
            inflated casualty of the quick reel
air bladder jutting past its teeth

calcaneus

the rudder bone, steering us with mercy
into our next steps over crags

worn smooth as the rolled grey

bellies of sandstone lipping

the sea at Drumbeg, barnacle-pocked,
slow as time. this hinge

of foot to grass, to gravel, where the body
separates temporarily from earth, last

part that remembers
chalky cliff, remnants of Dover

and tectonic shift, plates moving
apart and back again before dinner,
click your heels, bring us home

phalanx

time distillates until I'm nineteen
in my old blue room, ballet shoes

hanging retired, steps measured
in chalk and blood, same arthritic

oaks out the window but
everyone else still older,

bodies breaking into age. school friends
raise children down the block, keep

their thin fingers free of dirt, of flame,
the dog's mouth, this is a new deep fear,

what replicates can be undone,
unstitched, they buoy hope in

writing, *bless this home* etc., letters
curled onto reclaimed wood, they point
        and point

cuboid

it helps us resist the pull, that
stumble, we're tethered to

the present but lured by storyline,
mind leaping from calf cramp

to aneurysm, sunburn to skin cancer, hooked
on happenstance, the perpetual falling.

this bone feels the wind-storm
coming, holds stories old but untrue, wrecks

the sailboat on reefs unseen
at high tide, uprights it at the low,

tips us back on balance
trips us forward in to dream

metatarsal

we bait the crab trap with angel wings,
cast a remedy for doubt, I flip

the tarot to find the Empress glaring
back, a mirror, the moon, however

we can cling one image to another,
bone connecting bone, magpies

with an eye for the glimmer, lost
marble, bottle shard, labradorite

earring clasping northern lights under
stone, what stretches us from this

island to the next, trolling through
the bardo with herring whirling

unbitten on the line, leaps of silver through
blue fooling nothing—until we

nail down the veil of figuration, stab
holes into cat-food cans, zip-tie to

prawn nets, four hours later pull 200
mud-bugs skittering into the boat

cuneiform

mosquito bite, thistle scratch,
loose husk of a blister flapping

from the left pinky, summer
callouses roughening efflorescent,

moulting white off the heels, that script
of a scar where the stray carpet nail,

where the dog's uncut claws, that red dent
of last year's stylish wedges where

the unforgiving plastic strap rubbed
raw, this season's sandal burn

striped white, those signalling
wounds the flesh is heir—

navicular

we cross the photographed shadow of a woman
in cats-eye glasses and a two-piece,

a man cradling one glistening twenty-five-pounder
beside an outboard motor that chugged

them sixty years through black and white waters

into this frame. coordinates tattooed

on our backs, longitude of churches,
latitude the damp green places

we like to cry, twenty photos a day
of the view, we're another species

of wild mustard, adhesive vines and
a tendency to latch, we hang the backyard

on the living room wall, waiting
for this last bone to ossify, I find

my sister's writing, that peculiar slant
rising from the sea a humpback whale

breaching beside her kayak, causing her to lift
her dripping paddle and start to weep

JAMES

This city's occasional snow demands we slow down
five minutes more out the door into its muffling
unexpected crush. I have been slowing since July
since the small pulsing furl of him stopped in me.

Name chosen in a sunlit instant stunned with weeping
in the hospital room, only one heart left beating.
A boy the doctor tells us, right before
numbing my belly, before the still unwritable scene.

We had been saving the surprise, assuming
a whole lifetime of gender.
Back in the birthing suite this bardo of his body stilled
but still inside mine, the choice comes quick as all other

unchosen in those cruel bright hours between losing him
and losing him: between diagnosis, black and white
and relentless, and the long push that brings him
into this world, to exit him into this world.

I first float *Cedar*, the room holding us, the only
reality I can render, also that heady warmth—
then *James*, your middle name but not on our optimistic list,
wary of vulgar variations. Now he will never have

a nickname we cannot control. Agreed in a moment then
a sound quickly foreign in the social worker's mouth,
she's trained to name what's already lost before
he enters here. The name of a chance

(everyone thought he'd be a girl) now written
on the certificate of remembrance,
the hospital bracelet never meant to fit, all the bits
of paper they give us because we cannot keep

what counts. You steal the tape measure that held
each inch. The sky's off-white as a page.
Medical instructions: take it easy,
no swimming: that last too late, came after

I had dipped my bleeding body
in the ocean to remember the sweet swell he made,
loss traced in salt. We thought he left
this world unmarked save the trace of ash, footprints

inked and smudged and rushing their way somewhere else.
Time rolls out like the tide. Small drawers
of his imagined future shut. Two months old today,
I would have shown him his first snow, the quiet light.

My reckless imagination. We didn't consider
how this name would be with us a lifetime longer
than his, just ended: the name my mother will
have tattooed on her calf, the name my sisters

will remember to say, the name on donation slips
in memory—The quick hot guilt that rises now
when I think how swift we were in naming,
how incapacitated. But when his soft and silent

body arrived into this unsafe world, feet curved—
unwalkable and perfect—he looked like his name.

ENTERING UNCERTAINTY: REVELATIONS OF THE BLANK PAGE

LORNE M. BUCHMAN

(CHAPTER 2 EXCERPTED FROM *MAKE TO KNOW: FROM SPACES OF UNCERTAINTY TO CREATIVE DISCOVERY*)

You begin every book as an amateur... Gradually, by writing sentence after sentence, the book, as it were, reveals itself to you... Each and every sentence is a revelation. —PHILIP ROTH

No poet can know what his poem is going to be like until he has written it. —W. H. AUDEN

To know what you're going to draw, you have to begin drawing. —PABLO PICASSO

The literal and figurative blank page. We have all faced it. To some of us, confronting that ocean of possibility can be terrifying, filling us with doubt and anxiety. How will I conjure the first words of this novel? How will I break through? This vast, empty canvas—where do I start? How do I find the first notes for this song, its rhythmic structure? My client gave me a brief—how do I even begin to find the innovative solution they need?

Perhaps I should clean out those drawers in my desk first. I haven't called my mother in a few days. You know, I'm actually pretty hungry.

The first fundamental principle of make to know is this: We begin our creative journeys by entering uncertainty, a space brimming at once with opportunity and intimidating emptiness. That fabled blank page can be a painful, even paralyzing, prospect—but according to the artists and designers I've interviewed for this book, entering uncertainty, despite the apprehension it may cause, can also be empowering and ultimately revelatory. How, then, do we engage with that uncertainty? Where do we find the courage to enter the unknown, and how do we do it? What does that space feel like? What happens once we're inside it?

While conducting the interviews, I noticed that writers—of all stripes—are particularly skilled at addressing these questions, and in this chapter I focus much of my attention on their reflections. To deepen the conversation, however, I also weave in the work of practitioners in the fields of installation art, film, and screenwriting, and explore through that work several important nuances of what it means to enter uncertainty.

Writers quite literally know what the blank page experience is all about. In fact, they are often surprisingly accepting of the idea that they will feel lost for a while at the beginning of a project. There are countless analogies about writing, but the following description, conveyed to me by novelist and poet Dennis Phillips, is fairly typical: "When you begin it's like you're in the middle of the ocean on a raft and you don't have a compass, so you may as well just begin to paddle one way and not the other—because you just don't know where you are or where you are going."

In a 2017 interview, novelist Nicole Krauss reflected on her writing process and spoke about "the power of entering a space of the unknown." She actually described the experience as "calming," from which I gathered a sense of focus and readiness to embark on a journey to find, as she put it, "coherence on the other side." What Krauss finds calming, other writers experience as uneasiness. Either way, they all convey a central recognition and acceptance of entering the unknown and setting out on a journey of possibility.

Relevant here is the concept of "negative capability," coined by the Romantic poet John Keats in a letter written in 1817 to his brother about William Shakespeare. The idea has interesting parallels with the way many writers talk today about entering into the creative space of the unknown. Keats wanted to celebrate the artist or poet as one "capable of being in uncertainties, mysteries, doubts, without any irritable reaching after fact and reason." He deeply admired the capacity of the artist to create a thing of beauty that suspends resolution and accommodates ambiguity.

The idea of negative capability has found its way over time into the discourse surrounding art and poetry, and even into the social sciences. Baudelaire described negative capability as "an ego a-thirst for the non-ego." John Dewey cited the idea as having influenced his writings on philosophical pragmatism; he saw Keats's concept as a "psychology of productive thought." In the same spirit, the 20th-century British psychoanalyst Wilfred Bion saw the richness of Keats's concept as pertinent to possibilities of breakthrough and transformation in psychotherapy. He stressed the importance of the patient entering a state of the unrecognized and un-navigated—"without memory or desire." Similarly, Zen Buddhist philosophy speaks of the concept of Satori, variously translated from the Japanese as awakening, comprehension, understanding, or sudden insight. Interestingly, finding that moment can only happen when it is preceded by doubt and uncertainty: "The antecedent stages to Satori: quest, search, ripening and explosion. The 'quest' stage is accompanied by a strong feeling of uneasiness, resembling the capacity to practice negative capability while the mind is in a state of 'uncertainties, mysteries and doubts.'" In all these examples, the common denominator is the experience of discovery that comes from yielding to the unknown. In a space not readily defined, possibility begins.

Negative capability (and entering uncertainty) is not about passive resignation, ignorance, or insecurity. It is, importantly, an active pursuit. It brings to mind what philosopher Donald Schön has memorably called "an epistemology of practice implicit in the artistic, intuitive processes which some practitioners...bring to situations of uncertainty..." Many of the individuals I interviewed mentioned the creative potential inherent in being unsure. Some insisted that they needed it. But all emphasized feeling energized by the process of finding the way.

POINTS OF ENTRY

Your triggering subjects are those that ignite your need for words...
Your words used your way will generate your meanings... Your way of
writing locates, even creates, your inner life. —RICHARD HUGO

How does the writer begin? To borrow Richard Hugo's term, what are the "triggering subjects," the points of entry? I put this question to a number of different writers. It's one thing to enter a space of uncertainty, but what sets the process in motion? Is it a big bang? A small inkling?

The descriptions vary. A central life question will trigger some writers; a routine, banal idea will activate others. Entry points might come from a random observation, an isolated experience, an emotional stirring, a joke, a word, an idea for a narrative voice, a rhythmic urge, or simply "showing up."

Novelist Aimee Bender tells me that her point of entry is actually physical, not intellectual or emotional. "I write every day. I have a very firm structure; I simply commit to an hour and a half of sitting there. The joke—but it was true for me—is that the first time I tied my leg to the chair." The description of her process echoes the amusing and perhaps apocryphal stories about Victor Hugo locking himself in his study and writing naked. He would, apparently, give his clothes to his servants with strict orders not to give them back until he completed a substantial amount of writing.

Bender is more balanced in her practice: she simply holds the scheduled ninety minutes as sacred, writing or not. She needs to be physically present; for her, entry into the creative act is carving out time. "And I write down when an hour and a half will be up. And then that will be that. Later I read the essay on boredom by [psychoanalyst] Adam Phillips. He talks about cultivating boredom as a creative space. My writing really changed. I was restless. I was restless and bored but had this rule; the writing got much looser and stranger, and I got a lot of work done. And that has held me through all the books I've written."

The furniture designer and educator Rosanne Somerson echoes Bender's thoughts about boredom as an entry into creative space. She relays to me an exercise she has often conducted with her students to encourage new levels of discovery. She requires them simply to sit and sketch for an hour and forbids them to leave their chairs or to take any break whatsoever. Her interest is in what might emerge when the individual endures restlessness and even anxiety. She recognizes discomfort itself as a fertile context for ideas: "Our body is very adept at knowing how to prevent us from going into places that are not comfortable, so finding a way to get into that place when you are utterly bored is sometimes the most beautiful way to instigate a new kind of thought process, one that takes you into a whole new realm." Somerson is teaching a discipline of making, and she is broadening its definition to include showing up in a moment of uneasiness. It's another point of entry. The maker, like someone practicing mindful meditation, enters a space of uncertainty by setting up the opportunity to observe, without judgment, what might come through being present in the moment, even amidst (or because of) feelings of discomfort and restlessness.

In her TED talk on creativity, novelist Amy Tan asserts that she enters a world of uncertainty from a place of moral ambiguity which is, for her, a source of some of her deepest questions. She specifies that engaging a central question is her point of access. "I get these hints, these clues... and what I need, in effect, is a focus. And when I have the question, it is a focus. And all these things that seem to be flotsam and jetsam in life actually go through that question, and what happens is those particular things become relevant."

Poet and novelist Joseph Di Prisco speaks of entering with a simple notion or imprecise idea and then, through the act of writing itself, discovering a narrative voice that guides him, a voice that he conjures through the writing: "There is a way, when you are writing, that you find your narrator's story and his or her voice is taking you down a path. And you have to follow that. You have to listen to that voice. All the clues are there."

The story of how Tom Stern developed his novel *My Vanishing Twin* offers insight into his encounter with the unknown and his entry point into this mysterious place of creative discovery. "I simply began to write about a character," Stern tells me. "I'm always observing people, reading people, thinking about people, and trying to understand. I spend a lot of time trying to think about the difference between myself and some other person and how we wind up in the places we do." When he does begin the writing, no matter what observation triggered his search, he very deliberately tries to eradicate any preconceived expectations of where he might be heading. For him, expecting to manifest a certain idea (or even reach a certain goal) eclipses the make to know of writing. If he comes to the creative process with expectations, there is a danger that he will work toward fulfilling those expectations instead of remaining open to what the writing might reveal.

Amy Tan crystallizes this very point compellingly with what she calls "the terrible and dreaded observer effect." "You're looking for something," she warns, "and you know…you're looking at it in a different way, and you're trying to really look for the 'about-ness'… And if you try too hard, then you will only write 'the about.' You won't discover anything." Tan characterizes the creative process not as a search for something preconceived, but as a discipline that creates the conditions for invention. With *My Vanishing Twin*, Stern simply started writing about his protagonist. He wrote to get to know his character, to understand his behavior—all through the process, as he put it, of "moving words around," writing through it. In this particular instance, he discovered a character who was struggling with his own stasis, someone who had compromised just about everything in his life.

"Can you tell me why that figure was of interest?" I ask.

"I can't. I don't know why that was a compelling kind of character beat or note for me; it just was." He wrote pages and pages about this figure. And then, at a certain point, he began to think about what it would take to shock the character into some sort of new or different action in his life. That question of shock and transformation hovered for Stern but, eventually, he needed to leave the pages of writing and clear his mind. He needed to do something else.

"What happened when you left it, when you took that break?"

"That's when the central image came. I was sitting on my bed; my wife was asleep next to me. Just sitting there before I went to sleep, there came the image of this man who is pregnant with—a *man* who is pregnant! And simultaneously another image came to mind of this malformed, misshapen little person. And I remember initially thinking about the relationship between these two images—the pregnant man and the misshapen figure. And then out of nowhere the answer came that they were brothers. And I realized that I was looking at a story about a guy who was pregnant with his own twin brother. I was incredulous, saying that to myself. But I also remember another internal voice—'yeah, that's right, and now the job is to figure out what the hell it's about.'"

There is much to uncover about the process Stern describes. Quite obviously, he is wholly in that place of uncertainty when he begins. With an entry point triggered by an observation in the world, a question about a character, he finds himself on that metaphorical raft in the middle of the ocean. He begins to paddle in a direction, moving through the vast unknown to the known (or, perhaps more accurately, to a place of knowing more). His practice brings him to a pivotal point of insight not, in this instance, at a moment *in the midst* of writing but at a moment when he is doing something else—sitting on his bed, opening up a space for an idea to surface. There is creative power in a pause.

Repeatedly, the people I interview describe what amounts to a continuum of making that extends beyond the specific act itself, encompassing times when they are not (seemingly) directly occupied with the work. It is as if artists engaging in a project enter an expanded state of possibility. Insight emerges, sometimes, through the direct act of doing; other times it comes in retreat. Making, it turns out, is part of a spectrum of engagement. Discovery is not fundamentally something we can control; we can only construct the circumstances for its realization.

Both Stern and Bender insist on everyday practice as an essential part of the make-to-know experience. Stern tells of a pivotal moment in his career when he was studying under the great writer and teacher Elie Wiesel. In a one-on-one conference, Wiesel said to him quite directly:

"I'll give you one piece of advice. If you call yourself a writer and if you take yourself seriously, you will sit down every single day and you will make the time to write. And it doesn't matter if it's for twenty minutes and complete garbage or if it's for four hours of divine inspiration—you'll just write it down."

"That was twenty years ago," he tells me. "I've written every single day of my life since then."

The practice of writing in regular rhythm is itself a way into this world of the unknown. It is a kind of preparation. Some writers talk about writing as exercising a muscle. The analogy is apt. Writers get in shape with writing like athletes get in shape with their bodies. What is painful and inflexible at the beginning eventually becomes stronger, supple, even graceful. The discipline of writing every day is the training for all that may come. The practice is the preparation and is essential if a writer is to thrive in a place of uncertainty, a place of creative discovery.

Chris Kraus tells a thought-provoking story about how her epistolary novel *I Love Dick* came into being. The entry point into the world of the unknown was, for Kraus, a question about what she considered a failed career as an independent experimental filmmaker. When she completed her final film, *Gravity and Grace*, a project that she worked on for two and a half years and that required personal financial investment, she eventually had to face the sad reality that very few people would ever see it. Ultimately, it languished.

"It was the last film I made. After that, I swore that I would never make another film until I discovered why my work had not been successful. And so exploring that question became the work of *I Love Dick*. In my mind, anyway, I wanted to use myself as a case study to discover why my films had been failures."

What Tom Stern explores through the "triggering subject" of character, Kraus examines by way of her own experience. *I Love Dick* takes the form of love letters to another person. The characters are Chris and Sylvere (her then husband and longtime collaborator). Chris and Sylvere work together on love letters to a third party, Dick, who is Dean of Critical Studies at the California Institute of the Arts. Dick never replies to the letters, nor does he rebuff them. The letters just go out. "Writing on the silence," in Kraus's exquisite phrase—a variation on the theme of writing in uncertainty. Dick becomes a blank screen onto which Kraus can project everything, the *tabula rasa* of the imagined listener.

I prod her to go further. "Say more about how that fantasy listener functioned for you."

"It gave me a recipient, someone that I was talking to. In writing programs, they talk about finding your voice. I think what they're really saying is find your audience." By writing letters to Dick, she set up a structure that allowed her to talk to an external figure born of her own internal world, one that for her held certain cultural norms and limitations. In addition, she deliberately used that structure to create a self-reflexive dynamic. "I was determined to become an art historian of my own work. I wanted to take the terrible feelings of shame, failure, and humiliation out of myself and externalize them and look at them in relation to the culture."

"Did you intend *I Love Dick* to be a novel at all? Or was it just personal inquiry?"

"I really thought I was just writing letters to this person, that it was kind of an art project," she tells me.

Writing those letters became a discovery for Kraus that took place on at least two levels. The first was the encounter with herself: wrestling with deep questions of her artistic past as she wrote repeatedly and incessantly to this "perfect listener." But on another level, writing the letters led to the discovery of something larger that eventually took the form of a novel. "I didn't know it was a book until 1997," she says. By that time, she had been writing the letters for a few years. "I went out to the desert with years' worth of folders and copies of the letters. I rented a cabin and played with those letters, edited them a bit, shortened them. I began to shape them into the form of a book. The letters are what made it possible for me to start writing a book that became *I Love Dick*."

Courtney Martin, a blogger and author of several books, talks to me about her creative engagement with generative questions that confront her in everyday life, questions that serve as her points of entry. Like Chris Kraus, Martin speaks of how she navigates the personally unresolved and uncertain through her writing. She cites her weekly blog for the website *On Being* as an example of her process: in writing it, she often drives a variety of immediate and pressing issues to a fresh point of consideration. "It is about how I'm living my life. I'm looking for patterns. I'm looking for questions. I'm looking sometimes for just a moment that's interesting."

Martin is a journalist by training, and it is noteworthy to consider how she enters the unknown. She reflects that the journalistic process is typically one of investigation and reporting in the third person. Her inquiries, however, while born of cultural or political questions, are characteristically also deeply subjective. "A traditional journalist," she tells me, "would research something, write about it, but never use the first person. Never use the 'I.'"

This combined perspective in her work—the journalist and the personal chronicler—intrigues me. Martin is able to connect in a most unusual way big-picture issues with her own vulnerability, her life questions, her uncertainty. In the end, the conditions she creates for discovery in uncertainty, for working out her own thinking, for finding a way of knowing her point of view through the making/writing of it, is a product of both finely honed research and her own personal courage. Writing makes possible knowing something of the self. In the words of Martin's friend and mentor, the venerable author and teacher Parker

Palmer: "Writing is an unfolding of what's going on inside of me as I talk to myself on a pad of paper or a computer, a version of talk therapy that requires neither an appointment nor a fee." Richard Hugo, cited above, extends the point even further: "Your way of writing locates, even creates, your inner life."

In our conversation, Martin focuses on a project she is working on to elucidate her point further. As a mother of young children, she is wrestling with the educational options available to her family, wrestling with issues of class, access, and race in the world of public schools of Northern California. How do even the most liberal and open-minded white middle-class families make choices when it comes to the education of their children? "I'm working on a series right now about public education as an example of how white parents have been the obstacle to integration in many ways in public school systems." The question she raises is certainly pertinent to this moment in our culture, part of a larger societal challenge. Simultaneously, however, she is personally right in the middle of it all, struggling openly with us, with her own situation, with a pressing choice that she herself needs to make regarding her children. The combination is powerful and gives evidence of how Martin engages her creative process not just to know the product of the writing, but how she wants to live as well.

During a conversation about his poetry, Joseph Di Prisco offers a particularly unusual reflection about entering uncertainty.

"How would you describe your entry point into the uncertainty of a poem you set out to write?" I ask him.

"It's a rhythm," he responds. "It's a sound. It's music. Like I feel something and it needs to attach to words."

I love this response, which is unlike anything I have previously heard about entry points. "Can you expand on that?" I ask. "Can you describe the experience in more detail?"

"I have an unsettled feeling. I feel off. I can only discharge that feeling by writing a poem."

It is compelling to speak to a writer sparked by "rhythm" and "uneasiness," one who doesn't have a vision of the poem before he writes it but is compelled by urges, even yearnings. He stresses to me as well that, with his poems, he doesn't "have a case to make."

"I'm not telling the reader what I am thinking about. I want to make the sound beautiful or appropriate to the music/rhythm, appropriate to what I'm writing...I'm not trying to replicate anything. I'm trying to create something."

The distinction illustrates compellingly how make to know shifts our sense of the creative process. It is not so much the replication of an already known notion or vision, but an unfolding of an idea in the making itself.

BUILDING WORLDS AND COSMOLOGIES: A WRITER'S UNCERTAINTY PRINCIPLE

The important thing is that what we have...is an aesthetic of making rather than one of expression. —GABRIEL JOSIPOVICI

The value of nothing: out of nothing comes something. —AMY TAN

Having found an entry into this world of uncertainty, what then? What does the writer build within that space that moves the project forward? Amy Tan addresses this question by offering the idea of constructing a cosmology: "I have to develop the cosmology of my own universe as the creator of that universe." It is an environment for making, a framework, however mysterious, that allows the process to unfold.

Tan uses quantum mechanics to elaborate on her metaphor, "which I really don't understand," she confesses, "but I'm still going to use it." It is richly stimulating to think of the cosmology of creativity as energy and dark matter, string theory, particles, and a cosmological constant. It suggests as well parallels with Heisenberg's uncertainty principle, or the extrapolated reality that even the artist cannot know fully the exact position and momentum of the particles of the world they create. Tan needs to surrender to the cosmology of the created universe, even as she makes it. "You don't know what is operating," she explains, "but something is operating there." You can approach knowing only by engaging in it. Tan's exploration of her creative process centers on grappling with that enigmatic operation, playing with ambiguity, probing the mysteries— all through her "focus," or that central question she finds as her point of entry.

That focus, for the novelist, is the filter through which certain very specific issues become relevant. And with that emerging relevance her ideas have a chance to cohere and expand, and the writer suddenly recognizes persistent patterns: "It seems like it is happening all the time." And the making yields amazement: "You think there's a sort of coincidence going on, serendipity, in which you're getting all this help from the universe."

I spoke earlier of a continuum of making, in which creative engagement extends beyond the specific act of writing itself—sitting on a bed or stepping away. The pause. Chance and coincidence are examples Tan uses to illustrate that experience. The cosmology of her universe contains much that would otherwise seem random but, in a larger spectrum of making, appears purposeful.

"There are also things, quite uncanny, which bring me information that will help me in the writing of the book...I was once writing a story that included some kind of detail, period of history, a certain location. And I needed to find something historically that would match that. And I took down this book, and I—first page that I flipped it to was exactly the setting, and the time period, and the kind of character I needed..."

Tan enters a cosmology that is filled with opportunity; it carries with it the potential of chance, accident, the unpredictable. The creative process is undeniably, for many artists, that central experience of invention born of the seemingly random. "What are the things that you get from the universe that you can't really explain?" Tan wonders. "I have so many instances like this, when I'm writing a story, and I cannot explain it. Is it because I had the filter that I have such a strong coincidence in writing about these things? Or is it a kind of serendipity that we cannot explain, like the cosmological constant?"

What Amy Tan helps us understand is the beauty of yielding to the laws of a cosmology that arises through making itself. In that world, discoveries happen and mysteries unfold; the writer learns and accesses a different part of herself, unknown beliefs, ideas unimaginable before entering. "After being there for a while, and seeing the amazing things that happen," Tan explains, "you begin to wonder whose beliefs are those that are in operation in the world, determining how things happen. So I remained with them, and the more I wrote that story, the more I got into those beliefs, and I think that's important for me—to take on the beliefs, because that is where the story is real, and that is where I'm going to find the answers to how I feel about certain questions that I have in life."

Tom Stern echoes Tan's point: "Only by going through the various steps and stages will I ever be able to get to a point where it dawns on me that this point connects to that point, and I begin to see the shape of things. I have often found myself surprised that I didn't see those connections beforehand—why the hell didn't I see that? For me, there is no other way than through it to make those connections. I don't even know what the action is other than to sit down and move the words around and to work through it."

The very act of finding one's bearings as a writer, or exploring within the laws of a particular cosmology, can often unleash a sense of excitement and prolific creative output. Discovering the way through the unknown is invigorating. Dennis Phillips conveys to me that the very act of writing, of achieving a sense of direction (even momentarily) in an uncertain world, can open the floodgates. He fixes on that exciting moment: "Ah, I know where I am." And it feels like an epiphany, and then suddenly "the words are just pouring out in a way that feels like it's coming from without rather than from within. It's a wonderful feeling. It's an amazing feeling."

The experience Phillips articulates is not uncommon; many writers use similar language that suggests a feeling of something coming from outside the self, something the artist channels. Indeed, many describe what sounds like an out-of-body experience. This may be one reason why so many theories of creativity incorporate notions of divine inspiration. Other writers, however, explain that even though one might feel as if the force is outside of oneself, the act of writing actually taps into "another consciousness—but of the self," as Di Prisco puts it.

Similarly, the psychologist Adam Phillips talks about the act of writing as revealing surprises about the self, aspects of our unconscious that remain hidden until the making occurs. Aimee Bender adds a compelling insight: "If you are not surprised or you are not discovering, the reader will probably find the work to be flat or predictable." She cites the novels of Haruki Murakami to illustrate her point. "I can feel in his books a kind of intuitive movement. I can just feel it. And I think that's why I love them so much. And if in another book I find building blocks in place, even expertly moved, like Philip Roth, I can appreciate it and I can value it, but it doesn't go deep. It is a more distant appreciation, but it's not like it's rearranging my interior."

In her metaphor of a multifaceted and complex cosmology, Amy Tan offers an ingenious description of what might develop in the creative realm of uncertainty. Hers is a universe that yields both structure and surprise, the intended and the random, chance and order. It is a context that allows the writer to find both story and self (in a way comparable to Courtney Martin), an architecture of the imagination that reveals artistic form and personal depth. What is most significant about the metaphor in understanding make to know is how her cosmology emerges in the writing itself; it is something the writer experiences simultaneously as product and process. It's not unlike improvisation, where a thing made and a thing discovered are one (an issue I'll return to later). The cosmology in the making becomes the "cosmic theater" within which the narrative unfolds. The writer enters uncertainty but, having entered, finds an expanding universe of gravitational pull, dark matter, and exquisite light—all yielding the opportunity for deep creative invention.

Excerpted from Make to Know: From Spaces of Uncertainty to Creative Discovery, *by Lorne M. Buchman*

Make to Know: From Spaces of Uncertainty to Creative Discovery © 2021 *Thames & Hudson Ltd*

Text © 2021 Lorne M. Buchman

Reprinted by permission of Thames & Hudson Inc,

thamesandhudsonusa.com

THE DIALOGUES

NOAH WARREN
SIMPSON FELLOW

15

I sense a gray fear in the landscapes I move through, deep beneath the ferment of hormones and drugs and parties; burrowing toward it, I make it mine. The buildings I leave are gorgeous and neutral. They make me understand nothing in particular, which I am grateful for. I meet the people I talk with. Their stories stay with me a day then disappear.

We are accustomed to think of language as a supplement but it is a supplication.

An empty power plant. Vast speakers set in the walls rumble bass too low for the human ear. Instead our bones and teeth—the parts that will survive after us—receive it. Exactly two hundred people sit and stand around a large empty ring. Soon two dozen naked people, painted head to toe in gold, charge in from a far dark corner. They march in a circle and chant in their throats. They wear tall horsehair headdresses.

But we have seen art before, and guard against it. We don't expect to be changed and won't be; we know a fashion label underwrote the performance. But the golden dancers are *there*. Some parts of their bodies are impossibly taut and toned, others parts jiggly as water. And before the gold paint melts and runs off their skin in rivulets, they light the gloom like bullion. Their caresses are stylized but real. No one ever kisses. It is hot and chaste.

Later the darkness is absolute but we sense many, many bodies moving near us, rushing, breathing, though from where they emerge or where they are going we can't say. Later a corner of the German internet seethes with critiques of the performance, its Aryan tropes.

I stand in the middle of a soggy soccer field in Friedrichshain and the light, getting slant, wraps the long puddles and the short grass in ruddy gold. The word "squandered" bangs through my head and fills me with a wild crumpled freedom. I am about to turn thirty. My friends are swelling with new people or are reading the books that tell them how to, or why to, or why not to. It is obvious that youth is over, and that I am late to this knowledge. Like the crickets I have been singing when I might have been gathering, singing inside myself as I bike from district to district in the cold June night.

12

On the first day of what he called his Jesus year, Aaron drove up to Concord, took a tab of acid, and wandered out into the woods with a water bottle and his notebook.

An Eeyorish man, he was always getting broken up with or breaking up with someone. The last one was Nika, who, two weeks ago, had left him to go back to her climatologist husband, and was now in a bungalow somewhere in Tahiti.

It was beautiful and May. Pine needles sparked green against the blue sky. The oak leaves were fresh and crisp, finely spined, and the air that swam between them was soft with the last traces of the morning mist.

The Emerson of the essay's beginning cannot get grief nearer him. He cannot acknowledge grief any way but this.

Aaron's baseball cap, like the shapeless coat he always wore, was brown, with no writing or logos. Its oversize brim jiggled up and down as he walked. He had an ambling gait but he often stumbled on the uneven ground. When he did, the water sloshed around his Nalgene.

In the small dirt lot, his underpowered blue pickup ticked as it cooled down. A mattress and four blankets filled the truck's bed. There was a long yellow scar along its left flank, where, trying to back out of a tight spot in an underground Costco parking lot, Aaron had grazed a pillar.

We wake and find ourselves on a stair; there are stairs below us, which we seem to have ascended; there are stairs above us, many a one, which go upward and out of sight.

May: I might have been swimming too.

It was the first time I'd been to Seattle. Several times I biked out to Lake Washington with my friend in the early evening. The turf lakeside was thick, vivid green, and strewn with goose shit. In bare feet we ran back and forth across it, seeing how far we could still toss the rugby ball. At one point I tried to spiral it straight through the branches of a young maple tree. The branches swatted it down, and the ball fell, and bounced elliptically, unpredictably away.

The lake was so long and blue, and houses shone white on the hills of the other shore. I stripped down to my underwear. I expected the water to be cold. I didn't expect the lake bottom to be so entirely composed of rounded stones, over which a thin layer of scum had grown. They rolled beneath me as I waded out. I could barely keep my balance. Then I couldn't keep my balance. I let myself fall in the cold, shallow water. I banged my knee against a larger, upjutting stone, and cried out: *fuck*.

What opium is instilled into all disaster. It shows formidable as we approach it, but there is at last no rough rasping friction, but the most slippery sliding surfaces. We fall soft on a thought.

Back in Aaron's apartment, his sleeping laptop ran out of battery. The notes he'd taken for a decade, the first two chapters of his dissertation, and all the rambling voice recordings he'd made in the middle of night—sometimes high on weed, sometimes on Adderall, and sometimes sober—winked temporarily out of existence.

The way he described it, the famous pond looked new at dusk, and beckoned him irresistibly. But once he'd taken off his clothes and his glasses and started swimming, it seemed to recede from him. He was swimming through it, he was swimming through it, but even the water was getting farther way.

19: Experience

Where do we find ourselves? I had been lounging, reading on the grass of the park all afternoon, my friend had come and gone, as had the threat of a shower. Now the park was emptying out and the sense of time passing crept up on me. I had been lying down, staring up at the banded woolen sky. Then the sense of being left alone became a terror, and I leapt up from my blanket. Too suddenly: a cloud of stars, then darkness. I passed out.

I fell on my side because I remember, as I came to, as I opened my eyes, a stiff ragged clump of grass wandering in and out of focus, an inch or two from my nose. Around it, bare beaten dirt. Beyond it, more dirt, more grass clumps smoothing into the fiction of lawn. And my body—was somewhere. I was aware of my right foot, because it is often in pain, but between my ankle and my chin was a quiet white room. I was confused. I felt an inexplicable need to speak, but I couldn't remember any words. My hand tightened, I saw my fingers bend and press into the dirt.

Then I sat up slowly, carefully. The machine functioned, but the air around me was swarming with color. I batted my hand in front of my face. Nothing changed. I was sitting in the root of a rainbow. I was breathing the glitter.

To the degree I remembered I was an artist, who was supposed to live for experiences like this, I was happy—I was doing what I was supposed to. But in that moment that part of me was very small. I was scared. I had never fainted before. My *me* had never been interrupted so crisply, and I didn't know how much time had passed.

Beauty is hard to see when you're in it. And I had to believe this was beautiful. So I had to see myself as from across the field—a lonely figure, bright against the darkening trees. Yet when I opened my eyes the air was merely bright, just a little fluid.

I think there is a deadness in my gaze, a chill at the bottom of my heart. I have always wanted to be the person who could be transformed, but I wonder now, as I age and the skin of habit creeps over the milk of feeling, if *wanting* it was my error. What experience, what life, can answer the refrain of an unhappy and religious child: *elsewhere, otherwise.* Somewhere that child still sits like a judge, testing my ache against his, weighing in his soft hands the slowness of my change.

I know this moment will pass, and soon. It is like the freedom that floods in when you realize the conversation has become a fight, and could be the fight. The kind of freedom that rips away the habits of love and forces you to ask how much of the glowing fluid remains. Anything is sayable, everything is consequential, your heart crumbles but your brain glows, marshaling proof, deciding how much to lie, testing their every word for truth, recording every flickering expression of that face you know so well, understanding everything and nothing. And am I crying? Good. That means I'm vulnerable as I should be, as the script demands.

The freedom lasts maybe ten minutes, until the narrative arc settles back down on you like iron, or you become aware that it never dissolved. Then defense, repair. Words die into tone. The water has been churned and the huge waves will echo for days. You are both grasping at floating fragments. Sometimes when your fingers reach out they find some edge of the person, and grip it instinctively. But you can't tell the difference. Their limbs are wood, made things.

Some days I remember every terrible scene. Grief is a knot of tongues. A mess of rainbows spread above us as we drowned.

SIMPSON WRITING WORKSHOPS

ASPIRE RICHMOND COLLEGE
PREPARATORY ACADEMY (CAL PREP)

RYAN LACKEY, SIMPSON FELLOW

CONTRA COSTA COUNTY JUVENILE HALL: MT.
MCKINLEY HIGH SCHOOL

ALEX ULLMAN, SIMPSON FELLOW

GIRLS INC. OF ALAMEDA COUNTY (TWO WORKSHOPS)

DELARYS RAMOS ESTRADA & JESSICA LASER,
SIMPSON FELLOWS

NORTHGATE HIGH SCHOOL

NOAH WARREN, SIMPSON FELLOW

JOURNEY THROUGH LIFE

ANNA MORARU

I am like water,
Flowing through life.
I only move forward,
Gathering more knowledge and sight.

I crash into rocks,
I evaporate to the sky,
Sometimes I freeze,
But I always survive.

I am on a journey,
With no foreseen end.
I travel down the river,
Thought the soil and sand.

MISTAKES

ANNA MORARU

A paper is made,
And turned into a letter.
A paper is smudged with ink,
And sent to another.

The paper flew,
It rolled.
The paper got crumbled,   .
And burned.

It is still a paper,
Changed in its form.

MIKAELA PASALO

versātus

chlorophyll
(pronounced KLOR-a-fill)
brown, golden bronze,
golden yellow, purple-red,
light tan, crimson,
and orange-red

attached to a stem,
the main organs of
photosynthesis and
transcription, a flattened structure

at least that's what Google tells me.

the smallest leaf is the size
of a rice grain
the largest the size of a man

many people disregard the uses of leaves

a caterpillar sanctuary,
an aphid meal,

camouflage
for luna moths

or some shade for a ladybug.
maybe even a resting place
for bees
who pollinate

they flow in the wind,
fill our sky
and our floors

i would like to reincarnate as,
perhaps,
the leaf of a peach tree
just because
peaches are my favorite fruit

-vea

WINGS OF FLAMES

CRISTAL REYES-MORAN

1. You set her world on fire.

2. You left.

3. When the flames rose, she
needed hands to pull

her out.

You weren't there.

4. She withered.

5. She let them devour
    those flames

6. the last bit of hope
    inside her

    You weren't going to come back.

7. Inside her
    something ignited,

    sparking

8. her pain—wings, she
    flew

9. with burning flames; they
    match

    the burning sky.

PINK

VIVIANA VARELA

One of the most amazing things
about me is I love the color
pink. Pink means warm,
pink means memories,
pink is joy, is love.
Pink signifies breast cancer awareness,
I wear the pink ribbon with pride
because my grandma is still alive.
Pink is my childhood,
the big pink roses
we used to have on our front lawn.
It's the cold strawberry ice cream
on hot summer days!
Pink is my safe place,
my room and bed.
It's the sunset in the sky.
Pink are those of the lips I kiss.
One of the most amazing things about me
is I love the color pink.

AFTER & BEFORE

VIVIANA VARELA

After I felt empty, exhausted, and drained. After I felt ashamed and helpless. After I felt underserved. After I wondered how could I be looked at the same. After I questioned if he still loved me. After I felt hypocritical to even speak to him or ask for forgiveness. Guilt with a mix of conviction. I continued doing it. After I didn't put much thought into it. After it was like it never happened. But every time I go to him I'm reminded of the before. Before I was joyful with energy and there was time to spare. Before my inner thoughts were quiet and peaceful. Before I spoke to him freely and wholeheartedly. Before I felt forgiven and had no shame in asking for forgiveness. Even now deep down I know he's always loved me in the before and even more in the after because he is close to the broken hearted.

STOP. GO. NO.

ALISON ANDRE

Stop.

You're lying to yourself. You're fine. You're just being over dramatic.

Stop.

Your feelings are fake. You're craving attention. You're being a baby.

Stop.

Because you're capable, you're just choosing not to do it. You're choosing to feel this way. You're choosing to pity yourself. You're choosing to

Stop. Go.

Prisoner of the mind. The jail with invisible lines you chose not to cross.

Stop. Go. No.

No I can't. I can't go I can't start I've been stopping myself before it begins. Before I face what I don't know. What I don't know is scary. What I don't know is dark. What I don't

No. Go.

Go before it's too late. Go before you're stuck here. Go when you still can. Go before you

Stop. Go. No

-ing what I do now helps. Knowing I've done it before and I can do it again. Knowing the lies I've been telling myself are just that. I want to scream for help I want to scream

Stop. Go. No.

Stop. Go. No.

Stop. Go. No.

Stop Go

-ing in this loop wasting your life away. You stop. And you go. And I'm saying
No.

No I don't want to live in this cycle from happy to sad, energetic to numb, its a stop and go roller coaster and I want to get off. Im going to get off. I can't keep living like this. I know I can
Stop. Go.

and keep going.

GET BETTER SOON

LAUREN BAUSLEY

Your card is on the desk beside the box of matches.
I sit.
I pull a stick from the box.
I strike the red end against the desk.
Again.
Orange bursts from the red.
The heat burns my forehead, behind my eyes, and in my throat. My hand doesn't move. My eyes are still dilated, fixated on the flame. Even as smoke fills my nose and my fingers cramp and sweat, my hand doesn't move.
I bite.
I swallow.
I burn.
Your card is still on the desk. Matches in the drawer.

I should get better soon.

WARM SODA

MIA ALLYSON MONTIFAR

the taste of your kiss
like warm soda
on my lips
giddiness
floating to my head
drinking in
what's left unsaid
intertwining
my hand in yours
dancing
with the rain pour

held together by your
embrace
a most dangerous
safe place

what were we to expect
when you can see
destruction in retrospect

ignorant of the deep waters
we tread
reality keeps our wings
tied down with lead
the space around me now is
cold
with only memories

left to hold
lingering in my mind
　bittersweet
two people in love with
　lonely heartbeats

by the time
it was dawn
secret goodbyes and you
were gone
our hearts were always destined
　to break
and warm soda
　gives me a stomachache.

[UNTITLED]

CHARLOTTE FEEHAN

Your smooth, ink hair
Frames a smooth, pink face
Colored with our summer's ephemeral heat
(Which burns through
Your tempting
Cruel
White T-shirt)

Though my face is flushed redder than yours, of course
Because your slightly chapped lips and nape glinting with sweat
Are much too close
For this humidity

In July

We walk aimlessly
By blurred dreams and sidewalks
That sway from the sweltering concrete
(Our hands might touch as they swing by our sides)

I'm delirious, laughing
It doesn't matter if your joke was funny
Or not
Because either way I'll giggle
And hope my lip gloss hasn't melted off

I picked it because I trust you
Like the taste of cherry
Though your popsicle is melon-flavored
(Its juice trails
Down your wrist)
You don't care if your skin
Is sticky with syrup
I wet my lips
Taste cherry
Unsure what kind of animal
Claws at the hole in my chest

Your stride's pace grows, leaving
My stubby legs to try and trail you
We're almost to the corner
Where I suppose you'll say "goodbye"

Is it the end? But I thought
July had only started
I still see your hair
Your shoulders
(Which have only gotten broader)

I stop
Overheated, tired
There's so much effort just to keep up with you
Not to mention

The strain on my ribs
Because your chapped lips, white T-shirt, long legs
All squeeze the air from my lungs
(Tear my heart into two)

My foolish gaze finally
Drifts
Away from you

I choke back a scream

There is
A little, red thing
Lying dead.

It's a fox—a young, stupid creature
With bleary eyes and a coat too thick
For summer's relentless flame

Torrid tears spill down my blotchy cheeks
You turn, walk back to me
While your face stays smooth as ever

A hand pats my back
Dark eyes hold a grimace

I know you think
I'm ugly
As a dead fox when I cry.

ANXIETY

AMANDA DIMICOLA

I feel them all around. I don't know where they are. In the shadows, outside my window, hiding and coming for my family. For me? I can feel them. My heart pounding trying to figure out if I need to call for help. Would the cops even come. Is it simple paranoia? What is this feeling that hurts so much. I can feel them near, I can feel their want. I don't want to leave. I don't want to be alone. I need comfort. Where is my mom? I need a hug. I don't feel good. Where is my dad? I seek his gratitude. I feel my heart cramp. Where is my sister? I need to look outside the house and see if there are people there. Where is my dog? He shivers the same way I do fearing something that is shadows. They're coming for me I can sense it. I am alone, home. Everyone is out. It's raining. I'm crying. Covered in a blanket with my tiny dog in my arms. I need help. I need so much help. This isn't normal. Why does everything ache so much. Why does whatever I do feel fake. Is life even real. Am I real. Why can I feel the realities merging together. I need help. I'm on the ground shaking, crying, hoping someone will come to me the way they do in movies. It won't happen. I have a choice. Wait for the acknowledgment I need to get help. Or advocate for myself. No one notices me. I seek help. I talk to someone so kind asking for help. I still cry but I'm better. I feel better. I have medicine. I have a new life. I am okay. I no longer hurt. I no longer need help.

[UNTITLED]

SOFIA KOHN

The subtle sensation of her fingers hitting the table gave her the comfort she lacked. She was stressed about things most people never have to worry about. Despite being rather lackadaisical and free, something still holding her back. The house was quiet. The closet was sparse, but by choice. She didn't need much but was fighting for what she deserved. On her computer which lay on the table there were many tabs open. She seldom closed them after doing research or reading articles. Currently she sat reading an article in her post-minimalist furniture. It didn't look comfortable, and it didn't feel like it either.

When her right hand wasn't scrolling, she adjusted her glasses up her nose. Her left hand continued to drum a beat of betrayal all while reading the characters on the page. Though she was alone, she felt eyes on her as if the flies on the rough ceiling and the ants under the floorboards were crawling out to watch her. Even inanimate objects started to have eyes. The dishes crammed in the sink were watching her, the tall grass plant in the corner of the room had eyes on her. They were all watching, silently judging from afar. Perhaps the ants under the floorboards made her itch without control.

She lifted herself out of her seat. The plant she had noticed across the room looked dry. Standing up, she crossed the room and stopped in front of the cupboards. Her small wingspan was practically as large as the room itself. One of her wings reached up to the knob of the cupboard and grabbed a pale faux-crystal glass. Her hand drifted over to the faucet, having to yank on it hard to get much to come out. Luckily there was enough to fill the glass.

A buzz on the table caught her attention as she strode over to the plant in the corner of the dining room. She stopped in her stride and placed the glass down on the coffee table near the potted plant. She walked leisurely toward her phone next to her computer. With a couple steps she could see the caller ID. The flies on the wall were confused at her expression when she stopped beside the table. Her face gave away nothing at all. If anything, it looked like she was tired. She stood there for a ring. And then another. And then another. The voicemail tone beeped loudly once the rings commenced. She showed no sign of interest in whether the person would leave a message. She knew they wouldn't. They wouldn't take the time to explain why they were calling. They would make her find out for herself by calling back. Which she would do eventually when she was ready.

The call ended and she turned back to the cup of water. She bent down to pick the glass up once more and walked over. She studied the fronds adorning the stem of the sickly thing. Somehow the plant seemed to be rotting. She reached out to touch the leaves sticking out from the rest. Feeling them with her pointed fingers she realized that the plant was fake. The water wasn't necessary at all. Maybe the water itself was making it rot.

WINTER'S STORM AND JAMES'S SORROW

KAITLIN WEITL

paralyzed.

he was paralyzed. rooted in place. frozen in time. with nowhere to run to and nowhere to hide.

nothing could reach him.

nothing, nothing, nothing except those electric eyes. her eyes.

twin orbs the color of blue suburban skies. the color of the calm before the storm.

he should have known the storm would hit.

and maybe he did know. maybe he did read the signs. maybe he did notice the lightning strike.

the way it flashed across her features. the way it festered and sparked.

maybe he did notice the ice that began to crystallize in her gaze. notice the way that ice slowly chipped away at her warmth.

and maybe he chose to ignore it.

maybe that was his first mistake.

she knew in her bones it was too late.

too late to disguise her silent scream. too late to conceal the storm that brewed under her skin. the storm that raked its talons across her mind.

in all her agony, nothing could reach her.

nothing, nothing, nothing. not even those celestial spheres that he called his eyes.

twin suns, sweet as fresh toffee and painted golden like the promise of hope.

but sometimes promises are broken. sometimes hope is a delicate flame destined to fade into darkness.

like the darkness she was spiraling into now.

maybe he noticed. maybe he didn't. maybe it didn't matter. she told herself it didn't matter. sometimes, she thought. sometimes ignorance is easier. easier than empathy.

easier than acknowledging the storm.

like the storm that glazed over her eyes, coating them in a perpetual frost.

a frost that solidified into a verglas sword. and carved a hole clean through her, cleaving her in two. sometimes, she believed. sometimes it is easier to let the sword fall.

maybe, she thought.

maybe that's why he let it.

memories.

he was drowning in memories.

memories of her.

always, of her.

of her eyes. of her storm. of that one last moment.

he clung to them, those precious souvenirs of his past.

even as they began haunting him.

even as they began taunting him.

he savored the sorrow they sparked.

and did not even attempt to understand his woe.

all he knew was that he could not let those memories go.

she had tried in vain to conceal her pain.

from him. from the world. maybe, he mused, maybe even from herself.

but he had noticed. had watched it consume her. had done nothing to relieve it.

and that did not matter.

no it did not matter now.

not as he stood silently by and watched her take her final bow.

sometimes

sometimes she pondered the possibilities. the possibilities of his promises.

sometimes she found herself treading on the precarious tightrope of hope.

but then her grip would slip and she would double over and choke, succumbing to the downward spiral of her own self-loath.

succumbing to the savage scars of her storm.

and to the obstinate echoes of his ignorance.

it was better this way, she thought.

better for her, better for him, better for the both of them.

better that he just let her go.

it was not easy, though. she knew it was not easy for him to watch her go.

to watch her disappear into the winter snow.

STUCK

LILY SANCHEZ

A three-year-old girl, sitting in a dark, cold hole, no one, and nothing around

She didn't know that in thirteen years, she will be thinking about this over and over again

Scared and worrying thoughts go through her mind, not knowing what she was feeling

Alone? Or hollow? Vulnerable.

Not knowing that in thirteen years, she will be feeling that everyday

Whenever she told people that she had a certain recurring dream, they always told her that whatever that it was, it was going to actually happen to her later in life

She never dug a hole at the beach, she was always at least four feet away from a pothole

Scared of being stuck in a hole again, she avoided them at all costs…

not knowing that she was already in one.

Thirteen years later, she is stuck.

Scared of being alone *again* when she has **no reason to**.
The hole keeps getting bigger.
That little girl never had that dream again
because she's living it.

SENSELESS

BETHANY LEONG

Am I the villain in this story?

Hypothetically, yes but no

That can be an argument in and of itself that I really don't have time for

Maybe they do but that's not important

Well I guess I could get into some details, they wouldn't like it but who am I to care about their bull****

Sometimes I wish I could yank this clingy m****rf***er off my back

Maybe taking a knife, stabbing its useless soul from existence

If they weren't so…ugh, I can't even tell you how much I despise this a**hole

Everything they do, say, even breathe… I would do anything to get this b***h off of me

Well, not anything, if they really annoy me then just break it off, simple

It's not that simple unfortunately even if I wanted to end it all…they are a person with feelings, hurt, and reasons

Someone I wish to give a warm embrace and tell them everything will be ok

A person I can connect with pride and hate

That embodies me as a whole...

They are me

A FIREY DREAM

LIAM CASEY

From whence I came to this new city as a small innocent child. The place we stayed was what I called home for five years. I could feel the warmth of an orange glow as I lay in my bed. When awoke I knew that danger lurked and I must find my baby sister and parents. I looked in her room, in the play area, in the bathroom. I looked everywhere but she was nowhere to be found. The warmth grew stronger as did my fear. I was lost. My sister was gone, my parents, and my cats, too. It was just me, alone, in an emblazed home. The orange grew bright and the warmth unbearable. I cried out hoping someone would hear me and save me from my doom. But alas, I was alone. Darkness overcame me and I was back in my room.

A NIGHTMARE

LIAM CASEY

A man is standing in a queue. It snakes far beyond him and trails far behind him. He pushes his knees backward and forward impatiently. Then his legs begin to split into soft cross-sections of flesh. Like chopped vegetables, his body tumbles into a pile of neatly chopped chunks of tender skin and muscle. There are neither blood nor screams of pain, simply a calm collapse. He moves his dismembered hand and gently tugs on the pant leg of a stranger behind him and politely asks the man to reassemble him. With his eyes locked on the front, the polite neighbor carefully steps over the pile of scattered flesh. And the queue moves forward.

WHAT SHALL WE DO

AKIRA MARKS

At the door frame, I breathed in sulfur. What had become of that couch was a marvel for the most degenerate, gross beings in the universe. Man's sorry excuse for a man. With your denim legs spaced far apart—your head craned inward on your chest—you were fine with the lack of, and sudden, company. You seemed to be thriving on it, clearly, as decomposition should be a lengthy process, but your Hellish will prolonged this further. Your fingers became accustomed to the indents of various crusted-over stains etched into that couch. Weighted, your palms, too, encrusted themselves. You were poised like an unaware sculpture, standing proudly within spotless gallery walls as a warning. My hands were held behind my back in observation already. The plaque of your piece—*The Drunken Sailor*—shining with virtue found in its bronze. In reality, in describing your day trip, you had not mentioned your viewing of an art gallery! Nor had you mentioned my shift hours today. Nor had you warned of the woman.

You shitstain! Here you rot!

Little had you known that your head was supposedly facing the Heavens. A daunting popcorn ceiling domed your spirit in Room 408 on the fourth floor. I passed the threshold of hallway to living room. Look to your left, Sailor, as the third, fourth, fifth bottle tumbles to the ground. Number four shattered. I nicked my finger. Why did I stoop to gather the pieces? Your glass and aluminum colleagues either sat in mourning, in the divots where couch cushions should lay, or were strewn across the durable television stand. It was restitution for the Sailor. In the chance that you slithered through the grasp of Satan, resting beside your wasted carcass, I hope you beg forgiveness. Whoever in their right mind would offer you that satisfaction should join you in the Fire Pit.

I never offered that.

I allowed this! Fully, with what intention had been nailed to my hippocampus. Rusted over, sure, but piercing nonetheless. All it took was a violent hand to rip apart a withered steel fence and expose a bruised lump of neurons. Out of fucked-up tissue, why had my common sense still developed enough to see through red? You were years older than I, decades experienced, and exposed to gallons of blood in comparison to what now dried under your nails. You should know better. Your job was to make sure I knew better! On the other red hand, was it the emptied veins and photographic memory that eroded your morals? Am I defending an excuse of a man—one who denies their crimes even in death? Have I survived on the wage of blood?

I entered the bedroom.

That could be bleached to acid, yet stains would remain. Were you ogling at that king-sized bed still? Falling to your temptations in the face of inhumanity, just as you had today. Of course, today—last night, or however long you may have sat here—you have fallen to physical karma. How many times have you done that besides today? How many vacant bottles would have reversed your alcohol poisoning? I'm not sure why I bothered asking—you were never the counting type. Never as precise as my ignorance made you out to be. Imprecise enough to leave her pale foot uncovered. Stupid enough to leave her blond and rouge strands strewn about that pillow. I floated to her, and for some reason I felt as if my own blood replaced her's, which had soaked into that fine satin on the bed. I was shaking. I realized I was the only moving being in Room 408, and I was shaking.

You sick bastard.

I found myself at the heart of your eyeline. Oh, you sick bastard. What did you want now? My feet chained to wooden flooring as your slumped form stood still. Your eyes were unmoving. Watching. Waiting. I swear to God that bottle was rolling. It wasn't fair that you were still entertained. I had all the time in the day to take apart that bed frame, so I returned to the living room. You aren't powerful, and I had the power to be sure of it. I approached you—your eyes, my hands prying their lids open, could fully see the sheets. Even if my fingers' veins had dried, we would suffocate under an ashen landscape together. The paleontologists of next year would find us mid-ballet; the orchestral accompaniment of sirens and chatter conducting our breaths. Mine, at least.

But what partner you were.

What leader you had been. You earned a badge and everything! I hope you waltzed this woman to satin sheets to give her any sense of protection as you had promised the public you'd give. In hindsight, what good would a promise be? Many wordless promises had been tied between us in the past; most of which were broken once I stepped foot in Room 408. Once I got that phone call. When the door opened. I swore I locked it—or didn't hotel rooms have automatic locks nowadays? Lock or not, my fate was sealed once we first met, anyway. My nails slipped. Your irises flooded. I held you tight—tighter than any lover or stranger could. My back cracked into a hunch as my center of gravity assured that the first knuckle of my thumbs creeped well into your eye sockets.

"The eyes are the window to the soul"

A quote attributed to a handful of people: William Shakespeare, Leonardo da Vinci, the French poet Guillaume de Salluste Du Bartas. Historians cannot agree on a certain person, work of art, or sonnet to pinpoint the origin of the saying, so it will get passed around for generations as words, definition, and long-winded meaning. I will always remember this, though; how clever the stage actors are for memorizing lines via relation to an action. Yes, your pupils did shine a reflection of the painted headboard—oh, yes, that must have been the essence of your soul. If I am to lose my job today, by the hands of a murderer, then at least allow me to take the origin of an idiom. I, for one, know the impact of words. Words can mask intentions, mold the mind, and craft a podium for the speaker to be carried onto. My arms were tired—the last of my strength sent to my thumbs.

We were done for.

Flipped onto the ground, my head was held against the tainted floorboards. It hurt. Of course it did. I felt splinters poke through cotton. I watched our own coworkers flood the room. Like an activated hivemind, gloved fingers roamed the walls, floor, furniture, and bottles. I couldn't struggle—why would I? As the head of forensics took note of the two maroon divots carved into your face, my hands were promptly cuffed with thumbs facing the Heavens. The room was quiet aside from sirens and shoes. They all moved as instructed to, but I hope we'd all grown sick of the smell of sulfur by now. Still, I laid with splinter-coated lips as the woman's sheet was torn away—her eyes shut.

I spoke too soon.

My lids were wide open, but nothing could reverse my drunken state. The power you held, the urgency of their phone call. You could have smashed a bottle onto my own head and, half-lidded, I would have followed your stomps. It was over when it began! With every handshake, curt nod, and instruction—I was far into my fourth bottle. No, I had not killed this woman; yes, you obviously had. Do you see the issue? The universe does not take pity on me, no matter my good behavior or instruction well-taken. I cannot regurgitate what I had not known was alcohol till hours later. In my sobriety, I cannot offer the Heavens more than my bloodied thumbs—as I will offer you in Hell.

So here I rot.

ERIC

GABRIELLE NICOLAS

You are exactly like your father.

I hated those words.
Like my father.
Shuddered, as they shivered up my spine.
They didn't know what I knew.
We are nothing alike.

For he is fire.
Forged with unrelenting scorching heat.
Wild, persistent, blazing.
Hot coals lay in his belly,
broiled words,
bubble up from his mouth
and sear the skin.
If there isn't a path to be made, he trailblazes his own.
When he weaves across the ground, bridges go up in smoke.
Unyielding and destructive in nature,
Torched hopes turn to ash.
And when he roars, a house
falls to its knees.
I couldn't hold a candle to his inferno.

that was
until
It went out

only when his fire was gone, did I notice
the surrounding cold and
empty space

and how dark
everything could be

dense enough was the air to
stifle my screams,
every inhale turned sharp
piercing my heart
and leaving it out to bleed,

my frostbitten fingers turned raw
clawing at the frozen ground
begging the earth to bring back the heat

yet

in the wake of silence,
when the rivers of my eyes have run dry,
when my mind returns from its heavy slumber,
I think back to his form,

no longer blazing; teeming with life.
His belly shakes with laughter,
A sound so bright and full.
Eyes crinkling at the corners,
One line for every smile he's shared.
With worn hands, he wipes the tears off my cheeks,
Swaddles me in his heart's warmth,
And whispers softly
it's okay, I'm here.

You are exactly like your father.
This, I say,
I am.

Here is where I carry his torch.
Wild and furious,
and fierce and gleaming.
I could not feel his warmth,
Only remembering how my scars burned.
But you cannot know the tenderness of the fire
Without having first been licked by its flames.

And so,
my lovely dad,

You are here.
I forgot, and I'm sorry.
You're here.
All I need.
Is right here.

[UNTITLED]

MICHELLE ZYARKO

We took a walk late at night
You grasped my hand in yours
And sheltered it in your sleeve
We embraced clumsily as we strolled along
The streetlights akin to little flames
You always look pretty, but under the warmth
You become iridescent
We're alone together at last

Contra Costa County Juvenile Hall:
Mt. McKinley High School

I want to go
home

—B.G.

When I was born my mom was
incarcerated and I was in the
hospital all alone until my
grandmother came and pick
me up when it was my
time to go home to my
family because my mother
had to go back to
santa rita county jail
after she delivered me
and was ready to
be taken back to
her cell and think about
the newborn son
she just had

—A. W.

THUG EMOTIONS

You might be one of a kind but we all die the same

If you count to 100, would you still want to switch places?

Im going thru some thangs I pray its only phases

I seen niggas in they grave and I seen niggas get taken

I need a location shit getting shaky

I'm going in for all the ones I was raised with

Runtz in the wood Boi This shit so tasty

I only smoke cuz it take away the pain

Flashbacks in shootouts, high speeds,

we creep, kicking doors down

I guess I'm not somebody you can hold down

You told me that you love me

But you lied.

—M.G.

When that gate is open
When these chains are broken
Do I get loaded
Or get a job and stay focused?

—**B.G.**

I want to go
home

—**J.M.**

The preceding poems were written by four incarcerated young men at the Mt. McKinley School in Martinez, CA, between April and June 2022. I had the privilege of teaching a class on creative writing there for eight weeks as part of New Literary Project.

McKinley is called "Juvenile Court School" or colloquially "Juvie," but don't let the names fool you: it's a prison. I read Foucault's Discipline and Punish and listened to all the anti-recidivism podcasts: no political conviction or educational experience prepares you for what it feels like inside. Steel doors slam, surveillance cameras line ceiling corners, peeling paint, shit food. As a visitor, you witness these visible injustices that constitute the social death of incarcerated life. But the writing tells a deeper truth.

We had only a few consecutive sessions together. Classes were often interrupted by guards or sometimes abruptly canceled. Then a Covid outbreak at the prison forced us onto Zoom. When we did meet, we often struggled to find each other beyond the walls of difference. In a few moments, those walls came hurtling down. Poetry was the strongest dynamite.

Some of these poems were composed in response to prompts, some were dashed in the corners of the margins. All of them are published with the students' permission.

—Alex Ullman, Simpson Fellow

GOODBYE TO(MORROW)*

OLIVIA LOSCAVIO

What do I do

When your name is more common in my phone than the word "tomorrow"?

I cried in the bookstore while smooth jazz played over the speakers.

A granola dyke next to me talked about Kamala Harris's new book.

I wonder if she goes home to her

Granola

Dyke

Girlfriend

And they lie in bed together

Legs unshaved, no bra

Feminist literature on the bookshelf?

You didn't like to wear bras.

You thought you were a stud

But really you were soft.

You were my color purple.

I've always cartwheeled through the world bright pink

But being with you

Meant keeping my feet on the ground,

I think the grey from the pavement made me mauve.

I'm not sure what color you are anymore,

Because you wouldn't look at me on our last phone call.

I talked to the wall so somebody would listen to me as I said goodbye.

BEYOND THE PROCESS

RYAN LACKEY
SIMPSON FELLOW

Like most writers, I think, I'm hugely hypocritical. If anyone—friends, students, other writers, strangers—asks, I say that I believe in the lunchpail theory of writing, which holds that writing does not begin with magical, Aeolian inspiration, that it's not about finding the proper form to contain an amoebic blob of genius. Instead, writing is about showing up every day, about putting the butt in the chair and words on the page, about process rather than product—and a dozen other clichés besides. I say I believe this because I think on some level I do. As a model of creative work it's relatively democratic—and, crucially, it's teachable. There's no pedagogical model I've seen for manifesting inspiration, no syllabus that explains Orphic possession. But the lunchpail theory comes prepackaged with a whole apparatus of techniques, skills, and methods designed to make writing seem possible. Undoubtedly, they make the *teaching* of writing possible, at least hypothetically.

I say I believe this—and then I stand around, waiting for inspiration, wondering why I haven't written anything. When stunned by the realities of day-to-day life—politics, paperwork, email, Twitter—all I want is to be shocked into activity by an idea so obviously and overwhelmingly electric that it provides its own self-sustaining energy. I imagine leaping up, running to my desk, and clattering away at my keyboard—all this in a kind of blurry cinematic time-lapse—until I emerge from the fugue and reenter the world with something polished and publication-ready. This has never actually happened.

The thing is, the lunchpail theory has its own problems. Sometimes its emphasis on process sounds more like plodding, and there isn't much room for pleasure there. At worst it makes writing seem downright Sisyphean, and it's worth remembering not only that Sisyphus himself never claimed to be happy, but also that Camus never claimed to be happy while writing his essay about Sisyphus.

Emphasizing process just defers the question: if the point of writing is the process, what's the point of the process? What makes it worthwhile? Why would anyone want to reproduce in their own lives the image of the grim writer at the grim desk, every day, working grimly? It's almost gnomic or koan-like: you write because you write.

For me, at least, workshop is one way—maybe the only consistent way I've ever found—to break open process and find something inside that's worth holding on to. There were seven students in my workshop at CalPrep, a charter school in Richmond, California. All seven are girls, none are white, and they shared in the beginning a tentative enthusiasm about writing that seemed familiar to me, the kind of feeling that arises when you'd like to do something but aren't quite sure if you really can: a graduate student at karaoke, or a cat below a high ledge.

One easy story would attach to this enthusiasm and frame the members of the workshop—Mikaela, Alexia, Fernanda, Jasuara, Aquetzalli, Cristal, Janeli—as the energetic counterbalances to the stony process model, as writerly innocents whose ideas and fantasies haven't yet smashed against the rocks of reality. But that story, to my mind, conjures up a stereotypical image of the "beginning writer," someone eager and sincere but unsophisticated, in need of a robust grounding in form, craft, and technique. This image is unfair and untrue. The writing that came out of the workshop was both sophisticated and well-grounded; often it was beautiful.

The point, however, isn't that my students were already clever and accomplished writers before I arrived, although this is true. My goal isn't to distinguish my students, any students, as prodigies or adepts, unusually blessed by the spirit of genius that the process model (thankfully!) tried to abolish. The point is that workshop, at least for me, made possible a new experience of the everydayness that the process model champions but also drains of color. Ours was an everydayness whose emotional texture was not struggle or firm-jawed perseverance. To be sure, neither the 8:30 start nor the facemasked impossibility of coffee were always pleasant, exactly.

But workshop was that rare and underappreciated thing: an obligation, a responsibility, whose obligatoriness was part of its significance and its pleasure. Workshop was an everyday (or, more properly in our case, a biweekly) complexity—sometimes awkward, sometimes confusing, always exhausting by its end. It's no surprise: maybe the most legitimate writing cliché is that writing is emotionally and physically tiring. So is teaching; so is learning. All these, though, writing and teaching and learning, were done in collaboration, and this was, selfishly, the best thing about our workshop: the opportunity it offered for writing done in process, but done together.

At its best, our workshop didn't try to cultivate genius or produce tirelessly workaday writers. We didn't try to become new people. My students didn't become writers; they already were. Instead, together, we made writing the object of shared attention. Not aimlessly, not purposelessly. Not for the abyssal sake of writing itself, even. We wrote for ourselves, and we wrote for each other. We took the friendly and serious confines of the workshop as a focusing lens for particular acts of writing.

What I believe, with this workshop in mind, is that when we talk about process, we ought to have in mind a destination, a telos. We're always writing toward something, for someone, from somewhere. What workshop added to the process model was exactly this sense of emplacement, sociality, rootedness. If writing is about process, if the lunchpail theory is the best alternative to a rarefied picture of genius, then we ought to imagine process *in the real world*, you might say. A process that begins, in some cases, with the writer alone at the desk, but does not end there.

THE DAY I GRADUATED HIGH SCHOOL

MICHELLE ALAS

Her house had three hammocks in the garage and a parrot in a cage and mangos in the kitchen. She had pictures of her grandchildren on the chipped brick wall, facing where she perched on the couch every day. Each night, she prayed for each of her children, saying the names of their children as much as she could remember. If she couldn't remember, she would say "la niña" or "el niño."

When I would go to El Salvador to see my abuelita, we would take her out to breakfast. She painted her lips red and spread blush on her cheeks and wore her favorite floral-patterned blouses. She would not leave without looking her best. Breakfast was served as we would sit by the water or overlook a volcano.

I did not get to see her often. I used to go every summer, and in the summers the rain did not stop pouring. I began to miss the land of endless rain. The country where pupusas were made a dozen a minute on the street and the humidity was a constant sheen on your skin. I found myself going summer after summer without a trip to El Salvador, as the gang violence infiltrated my people. I found myself going years without feeling the embrace of the hammocks in her garage. Summer after summer without feeling her embrace, without simply holding her hand.

My mother went every year. My mother, the youngest of eight. The only child in the United States. I know that she was never quite free of the guilt, knowing that her mother was so far away, knowing that she could only do so much as she got older. I would hear about it every day. I would accompany her to send money over to El Salvador, the $100 she transferred across borders every month. I knew she wished she could be there instead.

My mother and father moved here for me. For my education. I hear it every day. For the schools here, for the opportunities here. Throughout my life, I have thrown myself into my studies, without pressure from them, but with the silent knowledge in my head that I must. When I think of my childhood, all I remember are days spent studying in a one-bedroom apartment, the home of three immigrants. Not a day went by that I did not wish for, as I liked to call it, a "real house." Our wistfulness led to hundreds of wasted lottery tickets and visits to open houses we knew we could never buy. I never brought friends home, afraid of judgement when just the street over were houses with three floors and a pool in their backyard. It was hard to ignore the knowledge that in El Salvador we had a "real house," with a stairwell and gatherings at home. A home closer to family, to my abuela. My family left behind the only home we would ever be able to own. So, I fell headfirst into my studies, always cognizant of the choice that was made for me. The choice that kept a daughter away from her mother.

My mother did her best. She would send the money and she would call the family and she would tell my grandmother that she loved her and that we would see her soon. And she usually did, about once a year, when my mother would fly to go see her in El Salvador. Every year, my mother would take her out to breakfast, to the restaurants that overlook the ocean. She would try to make up for the time she spent away. The last time I went was four years before my grandmother died.

It is easy to think about all that you would have done differently had you known. If I would have known that was my last time with her, I would have held her hand more. I would have kissed her cheek and told her how much I loved her. I would have spent more time next to her. I should have thought to do that then.

My abuelita was old, having had health complications for my entire lifetime. She had so much family that loved her throughout her long life, I was told. The pain she was going through was now gone. The illness was gone. But that did not make it hurt any less. That did nothing for my mother's guilt. Because she would go every year, but always feel like it was not enough. Always know that she chose to leave.

My mother left for me.

When Mamá Toya's health worsened, and her cane no longer sustained her. And her veins could no longer be found And her heart was beating far too slow. And she never slept, never ate, never closed her eyes, I saw exactly what my mother thought. She saw how she should have been there. With the rest of her mother's children.

As they were asking for forgiveness and singing hymns. As they were crying together, whilst angry at each other. She should have been there.

So, she asked for forgiveness over the phone. And my Mamá Toya responded, "Why?"

I could tell her why. I have answered that same question every day since the day I graduated high school. My mother could tell her why, too. Mamá Toya, I am sorry for all the summers we could not go see you. I am sorry for not hugging you enough or sending more pictures of my sister and I as we grew up. I am sorry for not calling enough or saying "te quiero" enough. I am sorry because my mother wishes she could have been there with you and asked for forgiveness in person. I am sorry because I know I am not the reason but it still feels like I am. Mamá Toya! Mira! Me gradué.

My abuelita died the morning I graduated high school. I remember waking up that morning to my little sister crying, as my mother held her phone in her hands. My mom kept saying how she wished my grandmother had waited just a little bit longer, had waited for my graduation to pass so my mother could fly to El Salvador and be with her. My mother missed her mother's death so she wouldn't miss my graduation. My grandmother died the day my mother's reason for being in this country ended.

My mother was at my high school graduation, hours before her plane to say goodbye would take off. As I said my graduation speech, I thought of what my mother had said: that Mamá Toya was watching over me now, watching me graduate in a way she never could have while still alive. And I felt her, I felt my grandmother with me on that graduation stage. I was on that stage because of my mother and my father and my grandparents and the family that came before me. I knew she was watching me with pride.

My mami now has other reasons for staying in this country. Her life is here, my father's job is here, but most importantly, my sister is in sixth grade. It is now my sister that my mother stays in this country for, and because now El Salvador seems empty. My mother tells me how now, with her mother gone, there is no reason for her to go back. There is only my sister going to the same public schools that brought my family here in the first place, for me.

My mother did go to say goodbye to her mother. She flew to the country with the rolling green hills and never-ending rain. She went to the house with the three hammocks and the parrot. She went to visit the mother she left sixteen years ago.

My mother went to bury her mother under a mango tree. The day after I graduated high school.

PASSENGER X

JOHN R. MURRAY

If you've ever chatted with white folks who had names like Spirit, Storm, Amaryllis, or Cloud; if you've ever enjoyed a lively chat about politics with a woman who had a long, white braid and a goatee, if you've ever encountered a weathered old hippie in a stained jacket who had a missing front tooth and a PhD from Yale; if you've ever had a friendly neighborhood housewife—the kind of woman who looks like she should be carrying a lemon cake to a church social—follow up an introduction by saying, "let me know if you ever need anything—flour...sugar...*pot*," then maybe you've spent some time on the Mendocino coast of California.

I spend a chunk of my summers in that secluded coastal area of northern California famous for its rocky coastline, old-growth redwoods, and antiestablishment culture. More specifically, I spend my time in Elk, a seaside town with eighty-four full-time residents where my family and I are kindly but cautiously embraced as "vacationers." The previous owner of the general store, who considered himself a refugee from LA, used to say, "welcome to reality," and although I won't say it's *more* of a reality than LA is, I will say that it's a very *different* reality.

It's remote; no chain stores, no traffic signals, no doctors, no schools, no cell phone service—you get the picture. Locals chuckle at *Patagonia*-or *The North Face*-clad tourists walking erratically around town, holding out their iPhones like divining rods seeking reception.

All this remoteness means that folks are a bit more connected to each other than they typically are in more populated areas. They know each other, they depend on each other, they give you stuff; they borrow stuff. They have expectations.

Which leads to hitchhiking.

Try telling someone from the Westside of LA, where I live full time, that you pick up hitchhikers, and he'll look at you like you just confessed some dark, salacious peccadillo that sometimes needs satisfying. You get a very different response in Mendocino where the anti-establishment culture combined with a dearth of well-paying jobs means that a lot of folks need a lift.

The logging and fishing industries were each, in turn, exhausted and eventually gave way to "growing" as one of the more reliable sources of income. The legalization of cannabis has been good for corporate growers but hard on small farmers who can't compete at the same level. The result of all this economic volatility is that almost no one is complacent about his situation.

This insecurity helps to create an ethos that frowns upon anyone who thinks he or she's too good to consider the collective needs of the community. One way this manifests itself is that people pick up hitchhikers, many of whom, by big city standards, look, well, a little sketchy. Still, in that particular culture, it's not surprising when the scruffy guy holding out his thumb on the side of the road can easily discuss anything from Chinese philosophy to String Theory.

Other hitchhikers are more stereotypical—they look fried because they are fried.

~

I was about an hour inland a couple of summers ago, heading from the coast to the San Francisco Bay Area to do some errands. The only way out is on a winding, hilly road through the redwoods and then the wine country of the Anderson Valley. The valley is sweltering in the summer, and the sharp turns and rolling hills often make it a punishing ride for everyone but the driver. On this particular Saturday afternoon, it was full sun and ninety-eight degrees when I rounded a corner and saw a man standing under an oak tree wearing a black T-shirt, baggy jeans, and a trucker's hat—his thumb in the air. On impulse, I pulled over and immediately felt the same combination of trepidation, regret, and then altruism that I feel whenever I stop for a hitchhiker. I lowered the passenger-side window and a blast of heat wafted in that made my eyes squint.

He picked up a backpack that was smaller than what most grade-schoolers carry, and then he reached into the bushes and grabbed a leash tethering a five-month-old, black, pit-bull-mix. They both ran toward the car.

"God bless you, man, thank you." He didn't seem that old, maybe in his mid-thirties, but he was missing his two front teeth. "Meth addict," I thought until I realized the teeth weren't rotted but broken off. This wasn't one of the closet sophisticates; this was one of the fried folks.

"I'm sorry, I told him, I didn't see the dog. I can't do it. I have a dog that will piss all over if he smells another dog." I wasn't lying; our dog looks for reasons to pee in the wrong place.

"Please man, *please*. I started walkin' from Boonville three hours ago, and no one has stopped. Please, please—I'll carry him in my lap; he won't even *touch* the car."

Hard-ass that I am, I said, "Okay, get in."

It took about eight seconds for me to recognize that this was going to be a difficult ride, but not for any dangerous reasons. The odor of someone who'd been walking in triple-digit heat for hours and likely hadn't bathed for several days before that infiltrated the car in no time. His dog's contributing stench brought it to a point of cruelty.

I wanted to roll down the windows—sacrifice the air conditioning for some of the stifling country air, but it would have been so obvious and so rude that I held back—he was polite; I wanted to reciprocate.

He told me he was heading to Las Vegas, where he was born, to replace his stolen birth certificate, which was one of the things he needed before he could replace his also-stolen license. Just as soon as he had that birth certificate, he was going to turn around and come back to California because Vegas was a very scary place, even though it was where he grew up. He'd seen some bad things. The problem was that he had absolutely no idea how to get to Las Vegas from Northern California, but his friends told him the 101 South was a good start, which I confirmed was probably right.

He said that the dog had been "rescued from some homeless people who abused it" (I didn't ask for details), and he vowed that he'd go hungry himself before he'd let it miss a meal. The conversation turned to the town of Lakeport, which he described as rough and unwelcoming, with lots of "dangerous homeless panhandlers."

So, I thought, are the stories of nasty homeless people his way of telling me he's *not* homeless or his way of telling me that he's in the constant company of the homeless?

We sat in silence for a few minutes. I drove; he cuddled his dog, massaging its paws.

As usual, ten minutes in, I knew that, in general, there's little reason to fear hitchhikers.

"I'm so happy to be in a car right now."

"The heat's brutal."

"That, too. I spent the night sleepin' in the redwoods, or *tryin'* to sleep in the redwoods, but somethin' was walkin' around us all night. Somethin' big—I heard sticks break where it walked. I saw pretty good 'cause of the full moon, but I didn't see what it was."

"Geez," I said, "sounds scary."

I thought of myself the night before, looking at the ocean, holding a glass of wine, gazing at the full moon, feeling that all was right with the world, but dreading my eventual return to the reality of relentless work and schedules and responsibilities. I thought of him without so much as a sleeping bag.

"Well, I been homeless since I was eleven, so I'm used to it."

There it was; he opened the door to discuss more than the heat or the birth certificate or the dog.

"Whoa, eleven? How'd that happen?"

"Well, my mom was a drug addict. She didn't come home for two weeks, so I just left."

"Geez..."

"I never knew my dad. The first time I ever saw him was when I was eighteen and he was in his coffin, so..."

I refused to offer up a third "geez," so we rode in silence for a minute.

Maybe he was working me, but I rationalized that this guy had been so vulnerable for so long that it didn't matter what he shared or with whom. He had his worldly belongings in a twelve-by-eighteen-inch satchel, his only family was a puppy, he slept on the forest floor, and he was missing his front teeth. How much more vulnerable can someone be to the rejection or judgment or scorn of a stranger?

"He was an addict. He was living with my grandma, and he went to California to buy drugs to sell, but when he got back to Vegas with them, he OD'd in her bathroom, so..."

"Did you grow up hearing stories about him?"

"My mother never said anything about him until he died. And then nothin' nice."

He said he didn't care what anyone said or thought about his father; he would have liked to know him and felt no anger or resentment toward him.

"Eleven-nineteen-seventy-two. I never forget those numbers. Eleven-nineteen-seventy-one."

"What's that?" I asked, my pulse rising at the first two numbers.

"His birthday. Eleven-nineteen-seventy-one. It might be seventy-two, I'm not sure, but I know it's Eleven-nineteen."

November 19. My birthday. I said nothing.

"Some things are hard for me to remember. I have a soft spot on my head, see?"

He took off his hat and tilted his head toward me, running his fingers across his skull, from ear to ear. His hair was only about a half an inch long and flattened by his hat and his sweat. There was a visible indentation along the crown of his skull.

"You know how babies have soft spots on their heads? I didn't have one, so they had to do surgery to cut a hole in my head when I was three, and now my skull has a big gap in it, but I've never had a headache in my life. After that surgery, my grandmother took care of me for two years. I'm hoping to find her when I get to Vegas. I stayed with her for a while when I was about fourteen, but that's six years ago, so..."

"So you're twenty?" Oh my God, I thought, he's only twenty?

"Yup, I turned twenty—two months ago. She might not want to see me, 'cause I ended up gettin' into trouble when I was stayin' with her. Spent a few years in juvy, but it was good; it straightened me out. Well, *juvy* didn't straighten me out—I made some dangerous friends in juvy, and two days after I got out and I was stayin' with her, I stole a car, but that's when I ended up in a youth camp and then from there in a really good rehab program for kids with no family—I spent a few years there, too. Those were good people and they took care of me. I worked there doin' maintenance even after I finished my sentence. 'Cause of those people, I'm not dead today."

"That's great," I told him.

Homeless, penniless, sleeping in the woods, and a soft spot on his head—and he still felt lucky.

"Hey, man, I'm sorry I smell. I know it's bad."

"Don't worry about it."

The truth was that the smell remained so potent that I was beginning to feel nauseated. The smellier truth is that I *was* getting on the 101 South, but my privileged, spoiled nose and I couldn't take two more hours of it. I lied and told him I could drop him off at the onramp, which was right around the corner from my fake destination.

As we neared the freeway, I had to say something.

"Did you say your dad's birthday was November nineteenth?"

"Yeah, eleventh month—that's November, right?"

"Right."

"Eleventh month, nineteenth day. So that's November nineteenth. I'm not sure what year."

"I gotta tell you, that's *my* birthday."

At that point, he put his hands on the sides of his face and folded slightly forward in his seat. "Are you serious? I can't believe this. Something's going on."

"Crazy, huh?"

He sat up again, pulled off his hat and swept his hand across his head.

"In Lakeport, I gave a homeless guy the only shirt I had because he was sick, and for two days, I didn't have a shirt to wear. Then I saw this lady in her yard, and I asked her if she had an old T-shirt I could have, and she went in her house and came out with *this*."

He pivoted in his seat and stretched out the front of his T-shirt for me to see "Las Vegas" splashed across the front of it.

"First that lady gives me this shirt that says *Las Vegas*, and then you pick me up and your birthday is November nineteenth. It means somethin', but I don't know what."

"Well, here's the freeway."

I turned onto the gravel shoulder.

"I really appreciate the ride."

I reached into my wallet and pulled out a ten and a five. "Here, have lunch on me."

"God bless you, man. Thank you so much. God bless you. God bless you." It was guilt money. His effusive thanks made me feel guiltier. "I can't believe that someone who has the same birthday as him picked me up."

"Crazy," I said.

"God bless you, man." He got out of the car, gently put his dog down, and grabbed his bag out of the back seat. Then he paused before shutting the door.

"You know, I'd like to be married. I'd like to worry about payin' the bills one day—that sounds good to me."

"Then it's going to happen for you, right? It will. Keep the faith."

Twenty years old, but I could see that it probably wasn't going to happen for him, and if it did, it probably wouldn't be for long.

"God bless you, man."

You better ask God to forgive me, too, I thought.

I was so relieved to roll down the windows and take a deep inhalation through my nose, but whether it was real or imagined, the smell stayed with me for the next hundred miles.

Hours later, my time with the hitchhiker resonated with me, needled me. Why didn't I give him the two twenties I had in my wallet? Why didn't I go into the trunk and pull some of the extra clothes from my own backpack to give him? For that matter, why didn't I pay sixty bucks and check him into one of the cheap hotels near the freeway for the night? He could have taken a shower and slept in peace with his dog, rested up before resuming his daunting quest to reach Las Vegas without money or directions.

But, I reasoned, I'd have to use a credit card, and what if he trashed the room? Stole something? Overdosed? If I lived in Mendocino County, it would be different, but imagine my having to explain to my LA friends that I needed to talk to the police about the homeless guy whose hotel I paid for and who was found dead the next morning...*right*.

We never exchanged names—perhaps because names were a superficial detail after what he'd told me about his life and my birthday.

There was a connection that seemed like more than coincidence—perhaps because he had no one and nothing—and only hopeful notions about a father he never knew.

As I headed south, I thought of that father, first condemning him, then empathizing with him. Did he think the big drug haul was the best chance he had for stability? Did he ever think about that kid? What went through his head as he lay on his mother's bathroom floor, the last synapses firing through his body? Did he know he'd soon be gone forever from someone who would have accepted him—in any state?

That father; our birthday.

I tried to convince myself that I did what I could for that hour's ride on a hot summer day, and that any of the locals would have made the same choices I did.

But I know.

I'm really just a vacationer.

JENNA TAKES THE FALL

A.R. TAYLOR

(Chapter 2 excerpted from the novel *Jenna Takes the Fall*)

Today, on this muggy day of June, after a remarkable few weeks of floating incompetently through reception, advertising, subscriptions (the biggest demotion of all), then upward into research, Jenna McCann occupied her desk at the center of an astonishing suite of offices, one of the most incredible in this opulent New York world. "Office," the word did not do justice to Vincent Hull's domain. How she had gotten here mystified no one more than herself. In her tiny hometown of Burton, Ohio, she was regarded as smart but clueless, mouthy, erratic, up for anything the wind blew her way, but lovely too, with mounds of light brown hair, beautiful white shoulders, sexy calves. She looked like a well-fed woman, curious but naïve, openly waiting, even asking for something to happen to her. After the death of her last living relative, her grandmother, Margaret Grace McCann, her art history professor at Ohio University had interceded with someone who worked at a New York art gallery, who in turn was familiar with the fact that Vincent Hull lost assistants the way a fisherman loses bait. So, why not suggest this rootless twenty-something who had had one or two menial jobs, in possession of a fairly useless degree, not actively evil to anyone's knowledge; why not recommend her for a job at Hull's somewhat tacky magazine, *NewsLink*, and give her a shot at the big wide world? Up until now she had had very few helping hands.

Each day Jenna's new job began the same way—opening up a bag full of colorful, misspelled cards, notes, and ragged clippings meant to insult or castigate her boss, Vincent Hull. These letter writers were the people who rarely could penetrate Hull's private email address, although if they did, an IT guy dealt with those. No, these were the Luddites with pen and pencil, with old typewriters, even pinking shears, sometimes using cut-out letters like writers of ransom notes, and boy did they rave. Today's batch contained worse, much worse, as she held up a thick piece of white paper onto which had been drawn a man dangling from a rope, with a Swastika upon his chest. Misshapen legs, arms, and a large male member stuck out from the torso. "Eww," she shouted over to Hull's other assistant, his real one, the executive one, Jorge Garza, a nattily dressed fifty-ish man with graying black hair, thick glasses, and a perpetual air of stern and deep thought. So far she knew nothing much about him except that he collected labels off the bottles of wine that he and his family drank, a family that consisted of his mother and a disabled brother.

Jorge came over to her desk to get a better look. "Shows a certain flair, I think, in the hatred department. What did you reply?"

"Dear Mr.—hmm, he only calls himself Sam. Dear Mr. Sam, Vincent Hull appreciates very much your interest in *NewsLink* and your views on its politics. He is committed to maintaining an open dialogue with his readers, and letters like yours keep that conversation open. Please do continue to let us know what you think."

"Send it up to Security."

"Okay, you're right, but I'm just wondering what a little kindness might do for this guy."

Jorge frowned. "We don't do kindness here, but at least you spelled everything correctly."

"I really can't lie to save my soul."

"Don't worry, that's a skill you'll learn here." He certainly did not want to tell her how the most recent letter-writing girl had gotten fired when Hull actually read one of her replies and then stood before this very same desk shouting at top volume, "You can't even fucking use a comma correctly. Your sentences just go on and on, typos, grammar errors. I sound unbelievably stupid. You sent this crap out under my signature? If I put a gun to your head, could you figure out the fucking spellcheck key?" He had shouted into her ear and then actually picked up a pencil and poked her in the forehead with the sharp end. The woman fainted on the spot, and only the resultant several weeks of heavy lawyering could get Hull out of the whole expensive business.

"'*Luxe, calme et volupté,*'" Jorge whispered into Jenna's ear now. "You and I need to create that here because nobody else is going to do it; no one else cares, so it's up to us. Luxury, peace, and—" but he didn't want to say 'pleasure' instead 'beauty'—"that's what we're going for. Some French poet, I forget his name, once described a room that way."

"Baudelaire."

"Holy god, at last someone who knows something. We've been a brain-free zone for quite a while."

"Ohio University, major in art history, minor in French. I owe it all to them, but of course I do miss my last job at the Internet start-up in Cuyahoga Falls. They were into porn."

"Maybe you could've gotten stock and become a billionaire."

"Not a fucking chance. Oops, no swearing around here, right?"

"Not by you and me, anyway." As things stood now, Jorge didn't want to burst her bubble about how thrilling this promotion from Ohio porn might seem. In fact, he wanted to clue her in on several upcoming difficulties, but didn't quite know how to start. When Jenna's phone bank lit up, he retreated to his desk across from hers on the opposite side of the foyer. Several feet behind them lurked Hull's inner sanctum, an office that resembled a large living room, several times larger than the apartment Jenna shared with two roommates in Gramercy Park. To its left was the kitchen and behind that the executive dining room, a small but companionable space. To the right of Hull's office, behind a perpetually closed door, resided a much smaller, "secret" office, entirely off-limits except to those invited in.

The mystified girl stared down at the buttons on the telephone console before her, all of which, all twenty of them, appeared to link them to the known universe as it stood today. One was labeled "janitor," one "executive editor," and another knob sported the word "Washington" ominously pasted beside it. Could "Washington" mean the President of the United States? This phone button? "Hey, I could scramble jets through NORAD. Let me think of people I can bomb."

"Now, now, these are early days. Power must be used wisely." Jorge folded a piece of copy paper into an airplane and lobbed it her way. No matter what the new girl said, she said it with a lilt, a bit of joy at the end of each sentence, and he began to feel better about his life.

A button lit up, and she punched one of the flashing lights on the magic machine, receiving only bits and pieces of someone shouting through a cell phone as if through shards of glass. "Yes, yes? Who's there?" she cried, into the digital void apparently, because now she heard no sound at all. "OK, if that was Mr. Hull, I'm totally fucked. Geez, sorry, my grandmother used to say I had no governor on my mouth, but I'll work on it."

"Don't worry, probably not him. He's been AWOL lately. " Jorge actually hoped the great one himself had finally decided to show up. Since late April, Hull rarely came in to work. He could often not be found; instead he allowed Jorge to do every single thing for him. Not that this executive assistant hadn't already had that function, but now the situation had deteriorated. Habitually his boss's feet rarely touched pavement. Cars, bills, appointments, phone calls, taxes, gifts, children, dogs, doctors, Jorge had handled it all. If someone had ever asked him, he would have said, "I live his life." And that he did. It was an odd sort of ventriloquism, but the man who takes up ownership of a big chunk of the world needs a stand-in, a dummy with a mouth talking but saying exactly what the ventriloquist wants that world to hear. At the present time, though, Jorge could no longer even find out what his lines were supposed to be. Constant accessibility: once upon a time his boss's mantra, but for several months he got only the occasional email, followed perhaps by a late-night phone call. If only people knew that almost everything in Vincent Hull's life originated with a bean-counting-type guy from Queens who lived with his agoraphobic brother and a mother with multiple health complaints. In another life he would have figured as the designated priest in the family.

Jenna's phone bank lit up again. A gravelly male voice announced, "I'm coming in," then hung up. Say what? Jenna held the phone out in front of herself and stared into its silent microphone.

"Okay, Jorge, that had to be him."

"Deep voice, authoritative, like an SUV crushing dirt?" Jenna nodded, but Jorge looked grim, staring down at his watch. "Jesus, I wonder what's going on? It's so late in the day, almost five. Go check out his office and straighten things up in there. Maybe dust a bit."

"I'll make it 'shiny as two dogs' balls under a bed.' That's what my Granny always said." In shock, Jorge could find absolutely no reply.

Jenna ran into the kitchen, got two towels, and then went back through the foyer into Hull's office, only the third time she had actually entered that room. To her art history trained eye, her so-far invisible boss inhabited an art museum. Chinese scroll paintings unspooled along mahogany walls, onyx statues with grimaces on their faces backed up against the four corners of a room that sported a marble desk the size of three dining tables. Colors were muted, deep green and brown, down even to the Persian rugs, all sumptuous, oozing importance and the luxury of a thousand choices. Outside of the Cleveland Museum, Jenna had never seen anything like this before, and it reemphasized the importance of the people who owned it, certainly of the man whose assistant she now was, no matter how temporarily. As she surveyed her surroundings and then the panoramic view from the windows, she could almost feel the rich man's cultivation of his contemplative self. The phone didn't even ring here; it lit up silently, to her eyes like a tiny bomb. Staring down at the flickering buttons, some coming on, others dying out, she hoped she had time to fix things up, though why was something of a mystery, as, according to Jorge, nothing ever got moved or touched except by Mr. Hull's wishes.

Jenna swept over almost every art object with the soft towels, including the fat, laughing Buddhas, lining them up evenly on the shelves. Books that had crept out of place got pushed back. She glanced at a few titles and saw they all related to current events, mostly written by notables who had signed the first page. A little too intimate for her, this private contact; as if she were touching a part of the man himself. When she got to Hull's desk, she found an antique silver frame that had fallen face down, and when she propped it up again saw a slender, dark-haired woman hugging two young girls in parkas, snow-capped mountains behind them. The family, no doubt, and she stopped a moment to see them better because they looked so happy. She closed the heavy office door behind her.

Before she could run out to primp, a skinny man with red spiky hair brushed straight skyward popped his head around the doorway. "Want some Shrimp Amandine?" It was only 5:30 in the afternoon, but perhaps dinner started early in these parts.

"Hmm, I don't know if I should." Jenna was hungry and anxious, but she wanted to please Hull's personal chef, mainly to score freebies she could take home. No gift too small in this, the dark-hearted city, so she took the plate and walked back to her desk, Chef Martin trailing behind.

Jorge smiled over at her. "You've got to watch Martin. He'll have us all fat."

"That is not true. My food is pure, no chemicals, no bad stuff, you will lose weight on it, I guarantee." Martin retied his apron and straightened his bowtie while he spoke. His voice had a foreign ring to it, but Jenna couldn't place the accent.

She rushed through the delicious concoction to finish before the great man arrived, and indeed within moments after wiping her mouth and putting on more lipstick, she heard heavy footsteps coming toward them. Jorge made a sweeping hand gesture that signaled, "Sit up straight." Down through the hall they heard people greeting Mr. Hull, subdued though these greetings were, and she couldn't pick up any reply from him at all. Hurriedly she wiped her mouth again, but not before a very tall man strode through the door.

He didn't look at her, didn't look at Jorge either, and she only glimpsed an impressive profile. He went straight for his office, waving a hand in the air like the conductor of an orchestra. All Jenna had really seen was the back of him, his black leather jacket and his blue jeans.

She looked over at Jorge uncertainly, who mouthed, "Just wait." Nervously she wiped her mouth again, afraid of stray Amandine, and for a whole hour she fretted, no sound from Hull's office, only the ominous little gleam of the phone lights. What should she do? Jorge always worked feverishly, but he barely looked up. At last Hull buzzed her—she knew at least that much about the system, and she picked up. "Come in here, please," the man said in a low, slightly less harsh voice than the one she had heard before.

"Right away, sir." To herself she made a face and then unaccountably threw her fingers up around her eyes like a pair of googly glasses all the while shaking her head at Jorge, who laughed. Just then Vincent Hull popped his head out of the doorway, surveyed her for a moment, and waved her in.

The powerfully built, tall man bent down over a package covered with customs stamps, bound with canvas straps, and he was trying to wrestle it open. Jenna thought maybe she should help him but was too frightened to advance, worse yet to retreat, and so she waited. The silence had just about gotten to her when Hull looked up and fixed his dark brown eyes upon her, what the Irish call "speaking eyes." His face was square, with a prominent nose and a high forehead, and his white hair curled slightly around his ears. This was the only soft feature on a big man who looked more like a well-dressed lumberjack than someone who ran a significant chunk of the New York world. He surveyed her and cleared his throat. "Do you like food?"

"I eat it," she said, a little too loudly, clasping her hands together to stop herself from fidgeting.

"Some women don't eat. Watch them at parties, they're figuring how not to actually ingest anything." He grabbed a box cutter from a drawer in the desk and began slashing at the carton.

"Oh, that wouldn't be my problem, as you can see."

Now he smiled, and it was a broad grin that made her sure his laugh would be even better. He sat himself down cross-legged in front of the box and began to root around with his hands. Out fell heaps of white Styrofoam popcorn. "Jorge tells me you're handling the letters well."

"I don't know, I mean they're pretty disgusting. Umm, could I help you with that, sir?"

"No." He pulled out the black walnut stock of a hunting rifle from the rubble of plastic and ran his hand along it. "This is part of a custom made Mauser 98," he said, and she watched silently as he assembled the pieces, several engraved with silver tracery. "What's the matter? Not used to guns in Manhattan? Or just guns period?"

"Not used to Manhattan, with a gun in it."

He pointed the amazing firearm toward the floor-to-ceiling window before them. "I could drop anyone or anything with this, and from a long distance."

"'When you're dead, you're dead, as dead as Kelsey's nuts.' That's what my Granny used to say. Nobody cares which gun shot you." Hull let out a harsh laugh in Jenna's direction and hugged the weapon to his wide chest. She forced herself to shut up. No chattering, another new mantra.

Certainly, she had never seen the makings of a gun quite like this, but she had seen guns. From her stepfather she knew deer rifles firsthand. He would spend hours cleaning his latest firearm from the Galco Army store, spreading all the components down onto the kitchen table, then working away with baby diapers and oil, while a grainy, bitter smell filled the house. This in order to take potshots at the rabbits and gophers out in the yard, one of whom he nicknamed Billy. He became obsessed with this one particularly elusive bunny, but he never hit anything whatsoever, though Jenna had lived in fear that he might.

"But you're used to food, as you said." Vincent Hull wiped his hand on his jeans and then stared at her again with those dusky eyes, and she knew he saw before him a non-New York kind of person. Plumper than her predecessors no doubt, with freckled skin, her hair bunched together imperfectly in a black barrette, today she wore a floaty yellow dress adorned with random daisies. It hugged her breasts, and Jenna could read the man's blunt assessment, but didn't move away from his concentrated look. After what seemed like forever, Hull cleared his throat, "I want you to take charge of the executive dining room. Jorge doesn't have time, and it's not rocket science, it's food and people sitting at a table. You check in with Martin every morning, Jorge will give you the list of guests, and then you call and confirm each one. He'll show you the menu. If there's anything that looks disgusting, that's where it'll get tricky. You'll have to handle that yourself."

"That's true." Any controlled or witty language deserted her.

"He's not an easy man." Jenna stood there watching as he continued to work on the stock of the gun, massaging it with a soft cloth. "Besides, there's not that much for you to do, and I'm not here as often as I should be."

"That's what I was told." She was afraid to say too much, though felt certain that she already had, like a fool.

"Jorge told you that?"

"Was he not supposed to?"

Now Hull just stared at her. "Okay, check with Martin tomorrow and see what's happening. He needs all the help he can get." As she walked out of the room, she felt conscious of how her body moved and that he must be assessing the dimensions of her rear end.

Jenna had been in the great man's office so long that, unusual for him, Jorge had stepped to the door to listen. When she finally reemerged, she almost ran right into him. "I'm sorry," he whispered, but she brushed past him to flee what she considered the single most baffling interview she'd ever had.

"I must be insane, talking that way. I can't believe he asked me to take charge of Martin. That's your job, isn't it?" She plopped down into her desk chair, fooling with her hair compulsively.

"Was my job, dear. I'm so happy. Never try to deal with a chef, just open your mouth and consume. Tell me, though, how did you get here?"

"By subway."

"No, here in this office, at this time. You're from Ohio, no?"

"Right, Burton, Ohio, but I have connections, or my art prof does. He thought I needed a change, and you know, 'a change is as good as a rest.'" Jenna gazed up at him philosophically.

"It is?"

"According to Granny Mac."

"My grandmother never said much except, 'Shut the friggin' door, you moron,'" but Jorge stopped himself from saying more, horrified at the cultural contrast between Queens and rural Ohio. Of necessity this young woman had to like him, because lately the mood in the Hull realm had turned even darker than usual, intensified, actually brought about by their leader himself, who, after years of being actively engaged, almost hyper engaged, now occupied some mysterious psychological limbo. He refused to deal with the editors and writers at *NewsLink*, hid out at one of his far-flung residences for weeks at a time, even while his family remained in the city, and when he did come in threatened bodily harm to his employees and then refused to acknowledge their existence, an unusual mode, since normally he charmed them to death or showered them with money after he had insulted them. It was ghastly, and Jorge had no playbook for this state of affairs. At the very least he needed help. Jenna was the first decent candidate for a job that was both menial and important, and he could tell right away that gratitude was high on her list of virtues, as after the first interview she had thanked him at least five times and also sent him a handwritten card.

TWO POEMS

RALPH J. LONG JR.

A LETTER TO PATTI SMITH IN ROCKAWAY

Patti

A photo of you drinking coffee in a café brought

back a Rockaway that has faded like a tintype,

memories untrustworthy, eroded. We came every

weekend to a stretch of sand that seemed ours by

right. Carrying cases of fast warming beer, we

sunburned in Speedos pretending to be fearless.

We wanted the iodined and oiled girls in untied

bikini tops seeking tans without lines. Afraid of,

rejection or falling for one who was not Catholic

and unacceptable to bring to our faith sworn parents.

Our limitations amplified when we walked the shore.

Gay men, not rich or buff enough for Fire Island,

stood naked among topless older women who enjoyed

our teenage stares even as we recoiled at their fallen

breasts so less exciting than the centerfold perfection

hidden in our bedrooms. Boom boxes competed with

Motown and Metal. Men who were just older flexed

to impress girls who might bring more thrilling nights

than those from distant neighborhoods. Bravado

swirled in contingents from Bedford-Stuyvesant and

Bensonhurst who were ready for a fight. That their

brothers were soldiers together, trying not to die in

Vietnam, meant nothing to those never called to go.

To the west was a gated place, the Irish Riviera,

Breezy, in the shorthand of home. One could see the

Twin Towers, architectural wonders not yet symbols

of loss. A retreat where cops, who hassled us for

drinking in parks, shotgunned beers with their firemen

brothers-in-law. An idyll away from the adrenaline

crushes of the city. We dreamed of belonging there.

Hope you have a good summer.

A LETTER TO LAWRENCE FERLINGHETTI
BEFORE HIS 100TH BIRTHDAY

Lawrence

What will archaeologists find after the San Andreas slips?

Titillating artifacts *a la* Pompeii or will a tsunami cleanse

the peninsula? The skyline offers no wonders, although,

I vote to salvage the Pyramid and Coit Tower. Jolting faults

do not linger long in memory, great denial follows temblors.

In all probability, this city of reinvention will haul the rubble

to Colma to be forgotten along with those already there.

Real estate tycoons will demand redevelopment over history,

selling the fantasy that the next big one is centuries away.

Thinking again about Pompeii, I hope more than cellphones

with Tinder apps and text messages in need of an emoji

Rosetta Stone survive or hookups will be serialized as the

pinnacle of civilization. The lives here leave few relics.

Wooden buildings and newspapers disappear fast. There are

no temples to 49ers; no shrines of solace for duped Chinese

living out bachelorhood in Gold Mountain. No one is left

who struck with Harry Bridges. Few who disembarked from

warships and decided not to return to the simple towns that

cheered them off to war, remain. Yet your Beat compatriots

are safe in libraries and the love generation thrills everyone

who dreams of sex and drugs and rock and roll. How will

gay men be depicted? After emerging into the light, disease

decimated a community and shifted power back to those who

wished the closet was still closed. Have you noticed the lack

of women in this note? di Prima and Johnson escaped me.

Feinstein and Pelosi, Steel and Tan force patriarchy to take

a back seat but, even here and now, women must demand

their worth. You have watched this golden place grow and fail,

argue and survive. Lately, it has boomed with gene slicers,

bankers and red-eyed coders, the types who dream of wealth.

Were people different that week when the judge freed *Howl*

and Sputnik soared? What would you preserve when nature

shows us our fragility?

Hoping they find the cable cars,

A LESSON IN DYING

DAVID WOOD

I awoke on the last Thursday in June and said to myself: "My wife's mother is going to die tomorrow." I was certain—the date had been set. She had contracted a doctor to supervise her as she took a cocktail of drugs that would induce a coma, then make her heart stop, and then, she would be dead.

And the next day it happened just as it was prescribed to happen. She said she knew what she was doing and signed the papers. She drank the bitter medicine, and two hours and ten minutes later, she was dead. The act itself was simple, but nothing about this process was simple or easy, particularly for family members and those close at hand.

I have always believed that a person has the right to choose their way of dying if it is possible for them to do so. I believed, to my core, that neither the state nor the church has jurisdiction over one's right to end one's life. It is a matter that should be conducted with those one is most intimate: the person's considered family, doctor, personal god—and, of course, oneself. I believed it to be a most sacred and serious right, to be handled with utmost dignity and care. I still believe that, but now I know—after this death, which did not take two hours and ten minutes, but was a process our family experienced over two years—that the toll it takes on those closely involved is difficult to measure. I know now, first-hand, that the costs on everyone involved are real and deep, tortured by all the ambivalences and contradictions that reside in our feelings—about personal responsibility and guilt, about family and the role of love, and ultimately, about life and death. To state the obvious, this is no easy journey, and certainly not one that anyone would choose to inflict on those they love.

I have come to see intimately what should have also been obvious: that the people involved in this drama play out the roles they have crafted with each other over many years. My mother-in-law would make herself the center of an extended family melodrama that, for all its inherent sadness, caused all involved pain as her desire to live or die oscillated back and forth for over two years. She played out the drama for everyone to see, and took them with her on each excruciating oscillation. Though she was resolved to do this thing, she was not one to go quietly into that good night. Her ambivalences and need for control came to bear heavily on us all.

~

My mother-in-law, Janet Garrison, was ninety-three years old when she died. A woman of immense energy, she devoted that energy to ruling and controlling her family, involving herself in and attempting to control every family decision. She was quite successful. To this day, my wife Kathy maintains that she would not fight with her mother because she knew, in the face of her mother's tenacious ferocity and potential cruelty, that a fight was never worth the pain it could cause. Her mother could not be wrong on any family matter, nor let one go. Now that her husband had died, and her children were grown, she had come to loose ends. For the previous two or three years, she had talked frequently about not wanting to be alive anymore. Possessing a flair for the dramatic, and not being immune to the cliché, she mentioned repeatedly to her daughter, my wife, of her wanting to fling herself off the Golden Gate Bridge. Her life was over, she was tired, she had no purpose and did not want to be alive. None of us could tell how much of this talk was real, and how much of it was a plea for sympathy or attention. What all of us could see, and what my wife felt acutely, was that her health and spirits improved when family visited. At those times, she would tell us repeatedly that she knew that we had busy lives, implying that she did not. Guilt—rational or not, intentional or not—ensued.

In September of 2019, Jan announced to her daughter that she wished to enlist the services of a medical aid in dying group to end her life. "All I do is sleep and wait to go to the bathroom. This is not a life. I am just existing, and barely doing that," she said, repeatedly. She sat in her corner chair of her one-room assisted living apartment, where she had moved two and a half years before after admitting that she could no longer take care of the house where she and her husband had lived since 1961. After Gary died in 2013, Jan had desperately wanted to stay in the house, and she was bitter that she could not manage it alone. She hated the assisted living apartment, often accusing them of everything from simple incompetence to malfeasance to price gouging. From that chair, she issued rambling diatribes that moved from excoriating the place where she was forced to live to bemoaning the fact that she was still alive. She said she should be able to end her life if she so desired, repeating again that she was not living a life. A month later, she and her daughter, Kathy, contacted Dr. Lonny Shavelson, then head of Bay Area End of Life Options.

~

I had known little about the legal intricacies of what we generally—and incorrectly—label "assisted suicide." I had a dear friend who, four years before, stricken by a severe brain palsy, had committed herself to dying by depriving herself of food and water, known to the medical profession as Voluntary Stopping of Eating and Drinking (VSED). Since Alice could not be deemed "terminal," she did not qualify for medical aid in dying. She could have lived for years in a continuing deteriorating condition, ultimately not being able to speak or swallow. She kept her own counsel, set a date to begin VSED, announced her decision to her husband and daughter, and determinedly followed through despite their initial protestations. The process took eighteen days, the last ten of which she was in a coma. Her family's pain and final ability to reconcile with Alice's decision was much different from ours. She did not waver, and as Isis, her daughter, said to me about the time leading up to her decision: "Alice just announced to us the date she had set for herself. Finally, I said to her, 'Mom, you are sprinting. Let us catch up.'" She also said that Alice did not want to see most of her old friends, and had asked them not to visit her. "She felt she could not live up to the person she had been for them," Isis said. "She did not want them to be disappointed."

During an initial consultation, Dr. Shavelson took Jan on as his patient, and seriously discussed her end-of-life options. He asked about her physical condition, her level of pain, and her involvement in the world. He received much the same rambling explanation that we had heard. She was tired (but not in pain), she rarely went anywhere because she could not get very far away from a toilet (she refused to use diapers) and she felt utterly useless and without purpose. His response was measured but pointed: he thought Jan was an ageist because she did not think old people were worth anything, and that they had nothing to offer. Furthermore, she was not, at this time, in a medically terminal condition. He could not ask another doctor to sign off on any procedure to aid her in dying, and he could not, in good conscience—even though he understood her wishes—"kill her because she peed in her pants." He said, more than once, that much of his practice was providing "options" for his patients to pursue as they approach the end of life. "I spend most of my time talking my patients out of dying." He told Jan that she was still his patient, and he would monitor her condition, and to let him know if her physical condition worsened. He would be present if needed. He kept his word, despite later having stopped taking on individual patients.

Laws which allow medical aid in dying have passed in ten states, as well as the District of Columbia, which cumulatively represents 23% of the American population. Most of these laws have been passed in the past ten years, and though there are minor differences in their details, the particular language and time requirements are such that anyone who wishes to pursue a medical option to die must meet the same criteria: the participating physician must ascertain that the patient is terminal and will die within six months, and they must have that diagnosis corroborated by a second physician, both of whom must then sign an affidavit to that effect. The patient must be deemed mentally competent and aware of what he or she is doing. The patient must verbally request the procedure and confirm the request no sooner than fifteen days after making the first commitment (this changed to forty-eight hours in January 2022 in California). Finally, the patient must be willing and able to sign the commitment immediately before taking the potion, and, most importantly, the patient must be able to "ingest," "take," or "administer" the medicine herself (the verb varies from state to state, and this impacts how the medicine can enter the patient's system). In all cases, this means that intravenous methods are outlawed, and lethal injection is absolutely prohibited.

After Shavelson refused to act on Jan's request, we spent a year in limbo. Jan wavered constantly and verbalized each ripple of regret or self-doubt she felt about her life. Kathy took her seriously and internalized each ripple. She dreaded going to see her mother, or even talking to her on the phone, never knowing which of her mother's voices she would encounter. Jan, at times, retained her sense of humor, but she could fly into a tantrum at any moment about her living conditions, the place, the anger she felt at being trapped in her body, and the injustice of being thwarted by a system that prohibited her from doing what she felt was her personal right. Kathy would recount the conversations to me at night while I cooked dinner, and I became increasingly angry while watching her continued frustration, due to never being sure where to stand with her mother, or what would set her off on another emotional rollercoaster ride that Kathy could not refuse to take. She felt constantly guilty for not being able to make her mother's life more full. I would light into Jan for how unfair she was being to her daughter, for involving Kathy each time she exploded in another temper tantrum. Not unlike a six-year-old child, she never considered the pain she inflicted on the one person in her life upon whom she most relied. I could empathize only with my wife's pain, not realizing at the time not how unfair I was being to her.

About a year later, things changed. Caroline, the hospice nurse practitioner, discovered a tumor growing in Jan's abdomen that she said would continue to grow and might eventually cause pain and death. We wondered if we should biopsy the tumor, and Jan responded much like the character in the movie *Bridge of Spies*: "Would it matter?" Since she would refuse any treatment, she, ironically, was right. So, Kathy contacted Dr. Shavelson again, and this time, he said that the circumstances had changed, and he determined her to be eligible for medical aid in dying. He said he would help her when she deemed herself ready. A doctor at hospice also signed the medical affidavit, and suddenly, Jan could determine when she wished to die.

Since she was not in pain, and still very lucid, the decision as to the proper time was far from clear. There were days, such as those when she would come to our house and sit in the garden, that she said she wished she could live forever. There were others, when she was alone, that she wanted to have the drugs available right then. As she had done with almost every decision since I had known her, Jan considered all of the reasons not to do something ("Well, I can't do it over the holidays, and then everyone's birthdays are coming up."), and so she wound up doing nothing at all. Meanwhile, Kathy kept hoping that she would go to sleep one night and not wake up. "Do you know how awful it feels," she said to me one evening, "wishing for your mother to die?"

∼

Finally, in May 2021, Kathy and Jan called Shavelson again; this time, to set up a date. I sat in the room while the two of them FaceTimed from the deck of her apartment. The Muzak station of light pop was playing an instrumental version of the Beatles' "Nowhere Man," and I smiled and listened to the conversation. Jan said, "I would rather be asleep than doing anything else. I am always tired. I am not alive." Shavelson told her some procedural things. She should practice swallowing four ounces of water, and the medicine tastes terrible. She would have to confirm her desire again the day he came to administer it, both verbally and by signature. He said he would have the drugs sent to our home, as he did not want them kept there or have the facility have any responsibility for handling them. They would arrive by way of FedEx and require a signature, as the package would contain 15,000 milligrams of morphine, digitalis, and some phenobarbital. "This should put to rest any notion people have of hospice workers killing patients when they prescribe a regular dose of twenty milligrams of morphine for pain," he said. "And please do not get stopped by the CHP and have to explain what you are doing with 15,000 milligrams of morphine in the car."

This took place on a Friday, and the package arrived the following Monday—dropped off on our doorstep, no signature required. The return address read "FG Pharmacy." I brought it inside, shaking my head. I have to sign for a wine delivery, and this death package was just dropped on my doorstep.

Still the rollercoaster ride continued, all of us wondering if Jan were "ready." Once, when Kathy saw Jan engaging visitors one day, she told Jan that she did not think Jan was ready yet, so Jan called and canceled.

The next day, Jan, who was upset that she had not gone through with her original plan, told Kathy that she had canceled because Kathy had told her to. Kathy retorted, "Mom, when have you ever done anything because I told you to?" Jan, for once, had to laugh at herself.

The next week we went to visit before going on a week-long trip to Southern California to attend our housekeeper's daughter's wedding, and to visit some wineries and museums. At the same time, coincidentally, Jan's hospice nurse and nurse practitioner called for their monthly co-visit, and everything changed. Caroline, the nurse practitioner, felt Jan's abdomen and monitored her other symptoms. She thought Jan's confusion would only increase as the tumor grew, because it might invade the liver, which would keep it from eliminating ammonia from the blood system and thus increase Jan's confusion. Caroline was worried that, perhaps, if Jan did not follow through with her plans very soon, she might not be able to carry out the medical aid-in-dying procedures. We called Dr. Shavelson once again and set the date for the following Friday. Kathy and I cut our trip short so that she could spend some time with her mother before that Friday.

~

The day itself goes off without a hitch. As a woman who spends most of her mornings in her pajamas, today Jan is dressed and ready, assuming her seat in the chair that looks out upon the pistache tree and the distant hills; the view that had occupied her waking hours for the past few years. The others gather: Kathy and myself, Jan's son Bill and his wife Bernie, as well as Jan's hospice nurse, Susan, and her nurse practitioner, Caroline, who Jan had invited and who said they are proud to be included (even though by the definition of their jobs, they cannot be there in any official capacity). Dr. Shavelson comes in, all business, setting up the counter where he mixes the medications and then sits in front of Jan, and talks to her directly. He asks her if she is ready, and has not changed her mind. She shakes her head, and she signs the consent forms. He says, "When you take these medicines, there is no turning back. When you take them, you will die." Without hesitation, Jan states that she knows the consequences. He asks if she wants to go to the bathroom. "You will not poop again for eternity." Usually, for Jan, getting out of the chair is an ordeal, her hands gripping the arms of the chair, rocking herself back and forth to build momentum so she could get her feet under her, always appearing as if she could fall back into the chair with exhaustion from the effort. Today she rises directly to her feet, and pushes her walker to the bathroom, saying as she goes, "Whatever you do, don't let them charge you for any of the damages in this place. I know they will try. Don't let them."

Dr Shavelson turns to us: "Not only is this a medical procedure, but also a social procedure. Survivors do not usually get to see the death of the loved one, to participate in the process." He goes through the physiology of how the meds work. He says that he uses a heart monitor to ensure death. "Once she has taken the meds and is unconscious, we wait. There are no rules."

When Jan returns, Shavelson asks her what she would like to say. Jan turns and looks at each of us, but then focuses on Kathy. "It is great going out feeling that the job has been passed on. Thank you. I love you dearly. Let's do this." Shavelson hands her the cup with the medicine. "This is bitter stuff," and Jan drinks it, again without hesitation. "You are right," she says, "This stuff tastes awful."

Kathy holds out a spoon. "Ready for your sorbet? Do not die with a bitter taste in your mouth."

Jan licks the spoon, then peers down and strokes her arm. "I feel crinkly all over, itchy in the throat." Then she is quiet. Shavelson says, "That is the morphine working. Sometimes a patient, half asleep, will reach up and scratch his nose." Then Jan is asleep, her mouth open, lips already turning purple. Her hands, rigid in her lap, began to relax. "It's like taking anesthesia before an operation," Shavelson says, "except you don't wake up."

He quietly leads us for the next two hours—part clinician, part raconteur, part shrink—all the while monitoring Jan's heart. We are silent, not knowing what to say or do, looking at Jan in her chair, a figure not unlike one in a wax museum, her skin turning a pale yellow. "You know," Shavelson goes on, "this is the only type of family gathering where I have never seen food. Think about it—every other family gathering centers around eating, bringing food. We are still working out what we do." He pauses and changes tone. "Jan's heart just stopped for about forty seconds, now it is strong again, about 120 beats a minute. We have some time to wait. One patient, who was ninety-three and a competitive underwater swimmer into his seventies, took eight hours—his heart was so strong."

Conversation started in spurts, mostly consisting of family memories of who Jan was: the remarkable strength of her liberal beliefs, her image of herself as a lone voice in the Contra Costa County conservative wilderness, then her unyielding desire to die on her own terms. Bill and Bernie wondered who to tell, and which of their friends may not understand or may be offended.

"You'll know when it's time," Shavelson says very softly. "Not explaining it leads to embarrassment—people see a healthy person one day who is dead the next. Telling people is a good way to get around the stigma. It's much better to tell them what is happening and get it over with, because it will come out anyway. Somebody will tell them. Families don't keep secrets." He checked the heart monitor again. "The wave on the EKG is getting wider and wider. The heart is poisoned. We will get there."

And we do—after two hours and ten minutes. There is little change as her heart stops. Dr. Shavelson calls the mortuary to pick up her body, and he begins to pack up the remnants of his work—the medicine bottles, his mixing utensils, and his gloves. He shakes everyone's hands, and says to Kathy, "We got her an additional year and a half. I think we did well. Oh, and though we get caught up in the details, please remember it is still a death." Then he leaves. Caroline and Susan move toward the door and wave goodbye. I believe it was Caroline who says, "I am so glad Jan got her way."

Her body sits in the chair as we wait for the mortuary car to arrive. We begin to load up some of Jan's belongings into our cars, so that the next day we can move her furniture into a storage space. We know she would not want us to pay for one more day in her space than was absolutely necessary. Each time I walk past her body, I feel an internal gasp, seeing her head tilted back, mouth open, her face slightly jaundiced, knowing that I am looking at a dead body. Ninety minutes later, the mortuary workers show up and take away the body. Rush hour traffic, they say.

⁓

Over the next six weeks I realized that Shavelson was right. It was still a death, and it remained a death with all its details: the sorting through of the remaining possessions of Jan's life, the attached memories, the ensuing tears of anger and guilt, the legal and financial gyrations and hoops, the laughter, and the loss. Kathy slept through days, lost weeks. I tried to stay quiet, to see what she needed, to cook us meals, to share stories and to plot out what she needed to do the next day. The details seemed overwhelming, and meaningless. Finally, after a few weeks, Kath came down one morning and said, "I feel better today. I think I can do these things." She was right: she was better, and she slowly proceeded, in fits and starts, the long, slow process of moving on.

⌒

Three months later, the first Sunday in October, we held a celebration of Jan's life attended by about forty people, mostly family and a few friends, none of them Jan's contemporaries, for she was the last survivor of her generation. No one mentioned the cause of Jan's death, since some people in the gathering knew and others did not, many of those deliberately not told, as family members feared that those folks would disapprove of Jan's decision. People made comments about Jan's power, the strength of her political and moral stances. Kathy read a poem celebrating Jan's voice, and I read one that she wrote decrying that there was so much for us to do, to change—and having so little power to do so. The ceremony was short, personal, which was—appropriate.

Toward evening, the eight or ten people left sat around the outdoor bar in Bill and Bernie's backyard. I sat next to a woman named Nettie, whom I did not know. She had returned to the Bay Area from Las Vegas after her second husband had died a couple of years before. She spoke of him as the love of her life, and of his painful death from a cancer that had riddled his body. She said he asked her to help him die, and she said in Nevada there was nothing that she could do. She had to watch as her husband suffered for weeks before he finally died. "I think that is the hardest thing I have ever been through, not being able to do what he wanted," she said. I told her then that Jan had chosen to get medical aid to die, and we had been there to help take her though it. She asked what it was like, and I briefly told her how it worked. The secret was out. I do not know if I overstepped my bounds, if what I said breached some family trust, but I think Shavelson was right: it will get out, and it gets around the stigma.

~

Today, about a month later, is the first real rainy day of the year in Berkeley as I try to reconstruct all of this, try to find coherent meaning for me in all this. Perhaps, at age seventy, I take experiences and place them in predetermined philosophical slots that I have created to organize experience—little changes my mind, and most serve to solidify beliefs I already hold. Here I believe, even more strongly, that at a certain age, an individual should be able to determine how they will continue to live, or if they wish to continue to live at all. Shavelson told us that almost all of his patients who participate in aid in dying do not "wish to die. They wish to live, but that choice was taken from them by an illness. They are not deciding if, but how, they will die. For most families, the problem isn't that the patient wished to die—the disease wished them dead." Jan's and Alice's experiences were the exception. What I have seen firsthand is the pain that this process inflicts on others, who have to reconcile themselves to the fact that a loved one is not only going to die, but wishes to die, and that all are involved in a process that runs counterintuitively to our most basic instincts. The living are forced to confront death head-on, not as an it-must-happen-someday abstraction, but as a real series of choices—and they must participate in these decisions, even if their choice is to remove themselves.

A few years ago, I wrote a sonnet to our cat, whom we chose to put down because he was in chronic pain. He was an old guy who had lived the first, long part of his life on the streets, and we took him in thinking we might be able to give him a good six months to a year. He lasted five years. I wrote:

> When Charley came to us, already old,
> He knew too well the habits of the streets.
> And he measured the world's dangers before
> He dared to move, knowing his life relied
> On stillness and silent indirection.
> Sidling next to car tires and alley walls
> He mastered the art of disappearance.
> Thus he, the litter's runt, outlived his brood.
> Here, safe at last, he remains slow to trust

Approaching food as if an enemy.
Now blind, slow, on stairs he will often pause–
Does he wait for death's shadow to pass by?
      Take time to notice—he has truth to give:
      Come up to death the way you learned to live.

I think of Charlie the cat now, as I take in the last five years and consider how both Alice and Janet chose their deaths in the same ways they chose to live, and how they took us on their brutal but necessary journeys. Each took the path she had to take—none other was possible, and we, as loved ones, were compelled to follow.

W. B. Yeats, in "Sailing towards Byzantium," writes, "An old man is but a paltry thing, / A tattered coat upon a stick, unless / Soul clap its hands and sing, and louder sing / For every tatter in its mortal dress." Old age takes everything from us, tatter by tatter, leaving each of us with decreasing say over our lives as each faculty diminishes. It is hard to retain our dignity and "sing and louder sing" for our tattered selves. In choosing to die these women sang louder for themselves. As Caroline said, as she was leaving Jan's room, "I am so glad she did it on her terms."

Finally, I can say, so am I.

STRONG TIES AND STRONG-TIES

KATHARINE OGDEN MICHAELS

(PROLOGUE EXCERPTED FROM *STRONG TIES: BARCLAY SIMPSON AND THE PURSUIT OF THE COMMON GOOD IN BUSINESS AND PHILANTHROPY*)

My first personal encounter with Barclay (Barc) Simpson—founder and prime mover of the Simpson Manufacturing Company, Inc.—was at the Barclay Simpson Fine Arts Gallery in Lafayette, California, sometime in spring of 1981. Upon knocking on the door of the gallery, I was met by a young man in a workman's apron who ushered me into a large room with white walls. I remember the sensation of walking out of the strong glare of midday sun into the gloom of the gallery, whose only window was the glass door on which I had tentatively knocked. As my eyes adjusted, I was first confused then amazed to find myself surrounded by fine prints, including ones by Rembrandt and Whistler.

The young man said he would let Barclay know that I had arrived. When he disappeared, I moved closer to the prints, trying to absorb the fact of their existence in this stark, unlikely place, a converted industrial building along a strip-commercial thoroughfare in a suburban town east of the Berkeley hills and the glittering expanse of the San Francisco Bay to the west. A few moments later, Barclay found me staring fixedly at the moody prints, etched line and shadow, pulled from incised, metal plates.

Looking up, I was greeted by a big smile and a resounding hello. He asked me if I would like to see the picture-framing lab in the basement as well as other parts of the collection. Here, I also met Sharon, Barc's wife, elegant in jeans with rolled up sleeves and a welcoming expression.

Before that day, I had only seen Barclay from a distance at a public meeting of the board of directors of the San Francisco Bay Area Rapid

Transit District (BART), where, as one of nine elected members, he served between 1976 and 1988. I had recently been hired into the BART Planning Department.

I thought myself to be an unlikely BART employee and I brought my own set of prejudices to the job. A bit arrogantly, I assumed that though the work might be interesting, I was unlikely to find many congenial spirits, used as I was to the company of literary scholars, writers, second sons, artists, waiters, gamblers and a wide assortment of over-educated and under-employed bohemians. Stunningly, at least to me, this turned out to be wildly un-true. BART—like all the places I had ever been before or since—had smart and stupid people, brilliant eccentrics and tedious dullards, as well as all the usual permutations in between.

That day in the gallery, I was meeting Barclay to discuss the convening of a steering committee made up of elected officials and staff from Contra Costa County cities along the transit corridor to consider the possible benefits of encouraging public-private partnerships involving the BART-owned lands.

Before my meeting with Barclay, I had been briefed by my boss on the various members of the BART board of directors. My memory is that Barc was described to me as a successful businessman, smart, straightforward, honest, fair, and rational. At the time, I hadn't yet realized exactly how rare that combination of qualities was in an elected official—or anybody. I don't remember if my boss also told me that Barclay was impatient—of wasted time, of pretense, of long meetings, of circuitous explanations, of the word "stress," of calculators, of wallowing and doomed pursuits, of long meetings. But whatever I knew about him in advance, when I knocked on the door of the gallery, I wasn't expecting what I found.

~

In August 2012, thirty-one years after I first arrived at that threshold, I found myself once again at the door of the gallery. This time, when I came in from the searing hot light, there were no prints left on the walls. The Whistlers had been bequeathed to the UC Berkeley Art Museum and the Rembrandts were in storage awaiting their eventual fate. Also vanished were the brightly colored canvases and installations produced by students from the California College of Art (CCA) and by professional artists from the Mississippi to the Seine which had intermittently graced the walls of the gallery for the thirteen years it was open to the public.

Barc met me at the front door with the same booming hello that I had known now for three decades. He led me through the gloom to his library, lined floor to ceiling with *catalogues raisonné* of the major artists of his and Sharon's collection as well as an assemblage of scholarly works on art and history. No noise from the street reached us in this cave, illuminated by a few desk lights bouncing off the colorful spines of books.

I had often furtively imagined the pleasures one might indulge if locked by mistake in this library with nothing to do but read and look. For all that, it was a simple room of modest size with none of the pretensions of a millionaire's library. It was a room in which Barc and I had scribbled notes on the backs of envelopes before heading out to some BART meeting or other; where we had poured over books documenting different states of Rembrandt prints when we worked together on the catalogue of their collection for the 1989 gallery show; a room in which Sharon, Barc, and I met from 1997 onward to discuss the management of an old, stone farmhouse in Umbria, Italy, which I had restored after leaving BART, and which we jointly owned; where I first took my husband-to-be, the writer Leonard Michaels, to meet them when we were suddenly engaged in 1996; and where I went, severely grieving, shortly after Lenny died abruptly in 2003.

Now, again, into this room full of shadows, I entered in high summer, a few months after Barc's ninety-first birthday. I had come to interview him. As I fumbled with the digital controls of the tape recorder, Barclay bluntly said he was worried that all of this might be a waste of *my* time. As it was to turn out, our conversations were to go on from that summer until a few days before Barclay died in November 2014.

His question from that first morning in 2012 hung over all these encounters: *Do you really think there is a story here?*

This was a question I had spent a lot of time considering. More precisely, I had been trying to get at what might be the value of the story to readers who did not know Barc personally. Though well-known to many businesspeople, universities, and the arts and education communities of the East Bay, Barclay is not a universally recognized household name like Warren Buffett and Jack Walsh, or, of course, Steve Jobs and Elon Musk.

He is not quoted in the Wall Street Journal or other business journals, even though many of the progressive business principles he exercised in the creation of Simpson Manufacturing make compelling reading for anyone interested in the unusual idea that the building of a profitable business might include the sharing of profits with a diverse employee base, as well as in finding concrete ways to make contributions to the larger community in which the business is embedded.

Against prevailing custom, Barclay managed to knit together the generally competing philosophies of bootstrap capitalism and the pursuit of the common good. Out of these often-oppositional forces, he established a professional and philanthropic practice based, for the most part, on instinct, largely without the aid of elaborate academic theories of business organization and management, or primers on how to be a good corporate citizen.

Yet for those who watched him in action as a businessman or collaborated with him on public-interest projects, he was a colossal, exemplary figure whose creed one might consider bottling to sprinkle on business and institutional leaders everywhere. Indeed, new business principles that closely resemble key aspects of Barclay's creed are just now, in the early 2020s, suddenly starting to erupt in mission statements at the highest echelons of American business in the form of what has come to be known as "stakeholder capitalism." Though Barc probably would have scoffed at the artifice involved in giving a glossy name to what he considered to be simple fairness and good business, he would have approved of the shift in emphasis from mainly bottom-line motivations to a broader definition of the responsibilities of business in relation to local and global communities.

Consider the lead-in entry on the Business Roundtable's website. "*On August 19, 2019, 181 CEOs of America's largest corporations overturned a twenty-two-year-old policy statement that defined a corporation's principal purpose as maximizing shareholder return.*" In its place, the CEOs of Business Roundtable adopted a new *Statement on the Purpose of a Corporation*, declaring "*that companies should serve not only their shareholders, but also deliver value to their customers, invest in employees, deal fairly with suppliers, and support the communities in which they operate.*" Echoing these principles, the World Economic Forum adopted as the theme for its fiftieth annual meeting in Davos, Switzerland, in January 2020, "*Stakeholders for a Cohesive and Sustainable World*"—a phrase which, even five years earlier, might have surprised its powerful and wealthy clientele. It remains to be seen how and to what degree these new corporate statements of principle will be transformed into practice.

Yet, something like what is now being called "*stakeholder capitalism*" was key to the founding and abiding principles of Simpson Manufacturing. These included Barclay's adoption of a radical form of profit-sharing for workers; health and pension benefits; on-the-job training programs that allowed employees to make a career at the company; tangible support for workers and their children in the pursuit of education and skills development; and a baseline recognition that families and communities are the life-blood of companies, not antagonists against which the private sector must struggle in search of domination. In this sense, Barclay represents an extraordinary story in American business—one that yokes apparently opposing forces by expanding the definition of "*value,*" while still making substantial profits for shareholders and stakeholders alike.

Still, publicizing Barclay's achievements is a tough undertaking, with no scandal or celebrity to spice the sauce. How to make a compelling story based on a modern model of virtue in the archaic sense of the word? I knew going in that Barclay would not be an easy interview subject, as he had always been intrinsically distrustful of self-exploration, of in-dwelling tragedy, or of celebrating past triumphs. For all his palpable mental and physical vitality—his essential openness to the world—Barclay was not particularly easy, or at all suggestible. There was nothing of the "pleaser" in him. Though full of feeling, he was never a sentimentalist, never a believer in rampant subjectivity nor in the psychological desirability of protecting people from brutal truth. Committed as much as anyone I have ever known to concerted action in pursuit of the common good, he was, nevertheless, a special kind of subversive, skeptical of popularity and consensus, strange in a man so likable.

Whatever story might be told of him—of his life, his family, his business, his philanthropy—this contradiction lies at its core. Or maybe this contradictory nature is just what they used to call "*toughness,*" before a public creed of personal sensitivities confounded the old virtues.

$\sim$

"Yes," I said, *"I think there is a story worth telling."* Turning on the microphone, I drew breath and began to ask cleverly oblique questions that I hoped would get at the contradictions, sources, and crosscurrents. I was pushing for the core, trying to pry under the lid of Barc's optimism, his stoicism—coming repeatedly at the same questions from different angles. Though I did snatch from oblivion a few very telling comments, overall, I was no match for his distrust of complicated explanations. Regarding the question of his own gargantuan success—as a businessman, a family man, a public man—Barclay was concise, the way he prefers it: his story could be summed up as being a matter *of good genes and good luck* and, as an afterthought, *being in the right place at the right time.* Trying to excavate beneath these conversation-stopping statements, I asked Barc how this innately deterministic explanation squared with his twenty-year financial support of a program to teach very young girls from low-income families to read and then to mentor them through twelve years of schooling, through college, and beyond. Surely, this is an effort to stem the determinism of severely constricted circumstances. Again, a short, undramatic response: *"You do what you can."* Barclay wasn't stonewalling; he was saying exactly what he believed.

Though I wasn't able to transform Barc into a gabby, self-regarding raconteur that day or afterward, I needn't have worried about any possible awkwardness between us brought on by my role of grand inquisitor. Instead, in the magical library, and later at his home in Orinda, along with Sharon, we enjoyed many hours of questions, digressions, and conversations enriched by the thirty years of our unlikely friendship.

～

That day in 2012, when I returned to the glaring sunshine outside the gallery, I was both reassured and rueful. Yes, certainly, this is a tale of good genes and good luck; of the extreme benefits of being a white, middle-class kid of educated parents in early twentieth century America; of enjoying innate physical and mental health; of coming of age as a businessman during the halcyon days of California and American post-war expansion. Yet it is also a story of something terribly elusive—what my New England relatives call "character"—that vague but vast, implacable set of personal resources and instincts that make all the difference in life. As impossible to pin down as the explanation regarding good genes and good luck, character is indefinable—but you know it when you see it.

How to get hold of that tale? And harder still, how was I to tell a compelling story about an essentially good man? As all serious readers know, the recitation of virtue followed by good fortune violates our deepest Aristotelian longing to be vicariously thrilled and instructed by the suffering and fall from grace of highly placed men. Even Pierre Bezukhov and Konstantin Levin must suffer great loss before redemption, and Prince André must die of his wounds. Even good men must suffer to make a story. And evil is, of course, always interesting.

It would be presumptuous and untrue to say that Barclay never suffered. The unadorned facts of his life include the suicide of his older brother; the bearing of the devastating news to his parents; the loss of many dear friends to war, disease, and early death; the breakup of his first marriage; the inevitable variable fates of his children and extended family; and a prolonged personal struggle against a disease that would win in the end, and not before delivering an exaggerated payload of pain. Yet, throughout this last, stubborn battle—as during his vigorous heyday—Barc firmly rejected the idea of letting suffering or melancholy shadow his life or shake him from his path. Indeed, he never spoke of his disease, nor would he allow others to inquire or sympathize.

This willful intention to move forward rather than look back is linked to the original problem at the heart of this narrative. Barclay never believed in belaboring the past, which is an unsettling obstacle for anyone trying to be his biographer. Though he was a great reader of history, he was never much interested in the details of his own former life, preferring to probe the concrete world of daily life, the future, or the impersonal world of great art and actions. Pure subjectivity was alien to him. Though interested in the psychology of the self, his concerns were cognition, learning, and motivation. Above all, he was insistent on viewing the self in relation to other selves, especially those battling great odds.

Knowing this, I realized that most of Barc's story would need to be told from the outside, not through his own reflections but through the actual facts of his life, and even more importantly through the stories of the people and institutions whose lives he changed so profoundly. One such person, John Herrera, who worked at Simpson Strong-Tie (SST) for over forty-three years, describes Barclay in terms of his *passion*, but struggles to explain precisely what he means by this slippery term:

> "Barc has the presence.... He's very intense. He's very direct. That intensity, though, it really is passion, but different from people who are just over the top. Barclay's words are very specific, very carefully used, yet he's not trying to sell you anything. He's not measuring or calculating. He just wants to make sure you understand.... So many men could fail by not identifying their limits or their passion."

Presence...limits...passion.... The weight of these words attempts to define qualities that are both concrete and inexplicable, that grapple after the texture of leadership.

Striking in the above description is the speaker's emphasis on communication and transmission, rather than manipulation or coercion. *"Barclay's words are very specific, very carefully used, yet he's not trying to sell you anything."* From this account and multiple conversations with other people who worked for and with Barclay over decades, what was to emerge repeatedly was the sense of how he managed by example and belief not only to "impress" people with his own passion but to "inspire" passion in them as well. The word "inspiration," from the Latin verb "to breathe or blow into," is often used in the sense of imparting a truth or idea to someone and was originally associated with divine or supernatural beings. Barclay was certainly neither of these—rather very down to earth—but he did have the unusual promethean power of imparting, igniting, and inspiring through his actions and convictions rather than through control, connivance, or false comfort.

After our 2012 meeting in the gallery, I knew I was looking for a way into the story that had character and the elusive nature of leadership at its core, but that would also tell a raw tale of tangible achievement—East Bay based, decidedly seat-of-the-pants, instinctively brilliant. It would be a story about the building from scratch of a small American manufacturing business that has survived and thrived from the immediate post-war era through the nineties and the severe technological and economic oscillations of the new century. The pieces of the story are complex and important: creation of a brand that now bears the Simpson name throughout the world; desegregation of plants and the unions that served them during the sixties and seventies, and early promotion of diversity in hiring and retention; establishment of plants outside of North America, while continuing to expand manufacturing operations in Canada and the US; development of a nonhierarchical company structure that attempts to have key decisions made at the lowest possible level; the fostering of a cadre of female leaders at the highest echelons of management (Karen Colonias, the second engineer hired by the company in the early eighties, is now celebrating her tenth anniversary as the CEO of Simpson Manufacturing, having shepherded the company to ever greater prosperity); recruitment of a board of directors that was at its inception mixed in race and gender; and carrying out a collaborative CEO succession at the height of the founder's vitality.

Perhaps most striking, given the current interest in business "culture," are the ways in which Barclay incorporated into the daily operations of the business and his philanthropy a set of principles that is a strange mixture of ancient Stoic philosophy, Scot's frugality, fairness, and twentieth century inspirational literature.

Yet, the core of the story is not the purity of Barclay's admirable precepts, but the rare skill with which he transformed precept into practice. In business, this meant that he never saw a conflict between making money and treating employees well, whatever their role within the company. He acted on his belief—certainly more intrinsic than schooled—that the greatest capital of any business is its people. To attract and retain both intellect and heart, the business must give people a stake and a future not based on dogged repetition of a task, but on cooperative problem solving at every level and across reporting lines. Matrix management at SST was never a theory or a theology, but rather an organic practice that grew up with the company, seizing on several aspects of the underlying metaphor encased in the word matrix, suggesting an intertwining of purpose that breaks the classic assembly line and recasts it as communal enterprise.

Though this sounds more like political manifesto than a description of the development of a successful manufacturing company, Barclay was no ideologue from either side of the political spectrum. He was a pragmatist who believed that making money and forging a community were complimentary goals.

Side by side with the narrative history of the business are the stories of Barc's public service, philanthropy, and art collecting, none in themselves unusual pursuits for a wealthy man. But, here, too, Barclay operated according to his own lights, rejecting the passive display of his wealth, using principles he had perfected in building the Simpson Manufacturing Company to better the lives of people and institutions. And so, back to the starting point: *Is there a story here?*

This is not a biography of a man from modest origins making it big. It is an attempt at a portrait of ethical leadership, which tries to analyze the structural architecture—richly symbolized by the famous Simpson Strong-Tie bent metal connector—that Barclay Simpson created in building important and lasting business, philanthropic, and familial relations. It is literally a story of *strong ties*, real and metaphorical, of the forging of economic, community, and family connections based on the careful distribution of force and burden. At the heart of the story are character and cunning, the mysteries that drive any great tale.

INHERITING MOM'S LISTS

IAN S. MALONEY

Thanks to Umberto Eco, I once started digging into lists years ago. I looked in books from Homer to Joyce, from catalogues of ships to Bloom's kitchen drawer. I bounced around Whitman's catalogues to Borges's "The Aleph." And then into paintings and enumerations. But, as much as my academic study moved through lists, catalogues, wunderkammers, and mirabilia, my studies led me back to my mom and into ineffable areas of home.

My mom's lists were infinite. Notebook after notebook of bound, ruled paper with nothing but things to do or jumbles of words she'd unscramble into new words. I look at them a lot now that's she's passed. I run my fingers through the pages to see how she lived: making things to do, writing out what had to be done, creating smaller words out of bigger ones. Often, the things listed were to be done by others. Mom checked out from a lot of the day-to-day work of living in her final ten years. We accepted that, even when it frustrated and angered us. We pushed back occasionally, tried to get her to be more engaged. Mom responded with a lot of sarcasm, a lot of sitting slumped in chairs and sleeping most of the day. Her life blurred day and night. She became less of the spark plug of her youth and grew more reclusive. Twice, she wound up in the emergency room over her last four years, followed by a rehab stint and promises to be more active. She often got what she wanted, and we gave in and loved her, even when we were exasperated with her and what had become of her life. She still never lost her sense of humor through it all, even when we did. She stayed sharp and witty, even as her world got smaller and smaller.

My family called our home the vortex, this green house in Marine Park, Brooklyn. Strange things happened there. It was filled with love and chaos and occasional magic. Mom and Dad were borderline hoarders—basements and attics filled with toys, memories, tchotchkes, and work supplies. They held on to things, collected things all their lives. Dad was an exterminator, so that meant rat stations, raccoon cages, and mouse traps. Mom worked the office, so that meant paper. Lots of it. She kept receipts, taxes, purchase orders, route cards, service tickets, paid and unpaid bills…mountains of paper. She just kept everything paper, from bill copies to birthday cards, from art works to essays. My sister and I kidded her often. We'd just repeat the word *Paper! Paper!* and Mom brushed us off as fools. *What do you know about running an office? You need to keep records!* Maybe we didn't know much, but we knew you didn't have to keep everything. Dad once called us pinko, commie, weirdos, but that was ok for us. The small-business, conservative exterminator and his wife/office manager raised two, left-leaning college professors, who learned what it was like to work Dad's job and manage Mom's business, even when we couldn't figure either of them out as people. They left a lot for us to look through, for sure, but very little to figure them out. We did know they sacrificed a lot for us and wanted to hold on to things that mattered.

We had a lot to sort through when our parents died. Lists of what had to be kept and what was ok to go. Ours was the story of so many families: make a checklist of what's to be salvaged and what's to be lost. Donate, repurpose, relocate a lot of what they held on to for decades. And yet, we retained mom's notebooks because they told so much of what she left behind for us, what we knew we had to do and particularly what stories we had to tell.

Mom's death came at the start of the pandemic. A cold, a cough, and then she passed silently in her chair in late January, clutching a tissue in one hand, with a pen and pad next to her. My mom died listing, in the same space my dad died twelve years before. They both died in the living room, ironically, staring at a stained-glass window, which brought streaks of red, yellow, and blue light into the space. They both died too young.

My dad always believed he was supposed to die long before he did. It was a miracle he made it this far—chemicals, ironworking, smoking, fighting, drugs, booze. He was fierce, like a lit fuse waiting to explode at any moment. He carried shadows from California and guilt over his older brother's death from a bad heart. Dad always said Uncle Donald was the good one, and his own mother asked God why he had taken Donald instead of him. My dad never left that behind, whether it was true or not, and he worked himself to death on the streets of NYC, seven days a week, until his body gave out on him. He lived his years, in some ways, like he was always on borrowed time.

My mom was different. After my dad passed a decade ago, my mom became a bit of a shut-in. She limited trips outside—she'd go months without venturing outside of her Brooklyn home. She taped a lot of things: news shows, *NCIS, Big Bang Theory, Modern Family, Saturday Night Live,* and the Mets. We joked that she was addicted to TV. Sometimes, during long marathons of her favorite shows, she would turn up the volume to drown out discussions. Many times, this was for shows she'd seen two dozen times. She could repeat the lines by now. We understood her reasons for staying in, while we wondered about her withdrawal. She was a Cancer survivor, and COPD took over her life. She stopped smoking Kools fifteen years before, but a good deal of damage was done. Her house was a maze of oxygen wires and a slow, rattling of the oxygen machine. The wires tripped you, seemed to slip their knots around everything and anything in their path. Many times, the family felt like it was in a spider web, with threads spun around every inch of the house. Hundreds of feet of green, plastic oxygen cord haunted us, almost cursed us, at times. My sister and I write and paint about this place. It was home, but it was haunted. That place keeps bringing us back, even when sometimes it feels you can't go home again. The images our parents left behind we carry with us today. Mom's shows, her cords, her endless lists. They spin onward into eternity for two kids from Marine Park, Brooklyn.

Mom's lists often bring us back to the green house. It always seemed like things were falling apart. Her lists were about plumbers, tax attorneys, gardeners, cleaners, builders, electricians, roofers, and yes, even exterminators. After dad passed, we had a visitation from rats in the pantry and a full-blown fly apocalypse. All went into the lists. Dad would be rolling in his grave with some of those. Mostly, the lists were shopping supplies, over and over again, with her necessities and favorite, odd little treats. I always pause and stop at Liverwurst and Pepsi, then move to staples like Muffins, Coffee, Soap, Tissues, and Toilet Paper. Most of the things there we had. She just wrote them again, in case we'd forget, or they got lost in the pantry.

But then, sprinkled into the mundane, like a lightning strike, you find lines like these: "*Start the dollhouses*"; "*Write the hijacking story.*" Mom kept these dollhouses for years. They grew dust upstairs. My dad would arrive with a paper bag from a place in Queens, and Mom had three he built for her. Tiny worlds, with intricate, comfortable furniture. Parents, kids, and pets collected dust without movement or change. For years, Mom planned how she would spend time rearranging them. All fell into disarray, but her lists show she never gave up on putting them back together. Never stopped thinking about reorganizing and repairing them. When time came to clear out the vortex, we couldn't part with them. Page after page of lists said the dollhouses needed tending, needed repair. We kept them to make something of them. Maybe an installation like a Joseph Cornell. A Wunderkammer. Or a Collector's Cabinet. My sister always finds new ways to stack them, arrange them, reimagine them.

As for the hijacking story, my mom, aunt, and their two friends were part of the first international hijacking in 1969. Flight 840 TWA, going from Rome to Athens, and then on to Tel Aviv, was hijacked by Leila Khaled and her accomplice, Salim Issawi, because Yitzhak Rabin was rumored to be aboard. The plane crash-landed near Damascus, Syria. No one was killed, but the plane's cockpit was blown off after the passengers were evacuated, and my mom and aunt and friends waited for the release negotiations through the Italian government, which had diplomatic relations with Syria.

Mom's life was hijacked. Literally. But, it's probably why my sister and I exist. It's probably why we're here to create things and tell stories. She came home after the hijacking, settled down from her jet-setting around the world and married Jimmy "Bugs" Maloney, who had also recently come back from a dark stint out in Los Angeles. They found common ground in seascapes, weekend getaways, nautical antiques, dollhouses, and love of family, particularly love for finding a way through disappointment, setbacks, and chaos. And somehow, it worked. Yes, it had its self-destructions and disappointments, but it also had grand moments of togetherness and triumph. In some ways, it's the story of my mom's lists: finding your way through the everyday, to find the extraordinary which gave you meaning all along. Or, maybe it's a way to make the extraordinary more ordinary, more in line with all these things we need to survive, understand, and move forward. Check them off as you make your way to the next story. Any way I look at it, that hijacking brought my mom home, to my dad, back to Brooklyn, and back to making mountains of paper lists, which now sit in my hands. That hijacking, and her lists, gave me and my sister life, both actual and artistic. I also think that's why we symbolically hold on to her dollhouses, for they keep her dreams of ordering, repairing, and rearranging a quiet, peaceful life, alive.

I guess I look at the lists as a reminder to tell stories that matter, when you can. Put things in order, otherwise, when you can't. Find a way to make sense of what you inherited, what you need to tell and what needs to be kept. My mom wanted to tell her story and find some order in a chaotic, difficult world. She repeated those lines *"Start the dollhouses"* and *"Write the hijacking story"* from notebook to notebook, buried alongside shopping lists and mundane things to do every day. Part of me inherits those stories and wishes we had more time to work on them together. But, a growing part of me takes comfort with her living lists and jumbles, of someone finding small ways to order everyday life, no matter how great or how small. Umberto Eco once said, "We like lists because we don't want to die." And maybe we make lists because we want people to know what we kept in order for as long as we live. Maybe those lists show what we wanted to repair, and what we imagined we could fix. Maybe the lists, ultimately, are how we learn what we lived for.

THE WOLVES OF CIRCASSIA

DANIEL MASON

2020 JOYCE CAROL OATES PRIZE RECIPIENT

The old man lived in a house with a wife he no longer knew was his wife, a son he no longer knew was his son, a little boy, and a woman named Seini, who told him each morning, when he asked where she was from, that she had been born in the island nation of Tonga. The old man, who once served as a physician on a battleship in the South Pacific, had been to Tonga and could recall, with clarity, an American nurse there named Rita—"like the movie star"—and when he told Seini this, his wife would stop and listen from a place he couldn't see. Almost every day, he told Seini about Rita—it was one of the many stories he told her. He had known this nurse only briefly, he said, and it was wartime, but often in the years that followed, he wondered what would happen if they met again.

"Who knows?" he'd say to Seini, and she'd laugh and answer that he must have been a flirt. Actually, the old man said, he had been a cardiologist.

The first time the old man had spoken about Rita, his wife had pulled Seini aside and explained that this story must be another confabulation. He had never served in the South Pacific, though he'd been stationed in Japan at the end of the Vietnam War. In fact, they'd lived there together. She didn't know where the story came from, or who this Rita was. To this, Seini listened with the same patience with which she listened to the old man. During the frequent moments when she was asked to take a side between truth and fantasy, she found she often chose the latter. She had been working with the old man and woman for only a year, but she had been a home health aide for patients with dementia since the week she had arrived from Tonga, and she knew with whom, on the deepest level, her allegiance lay.

The house was in Walnut Creek, in what the man had once called "Old Walnut Creek," to differentiate it from the subdivisions. It sat on a winding road lined with tall walnut trees, and had a small orchard of apricots and apples and a view of Mount Diablo. From the orchard, a path led down into a cool valley of oak and laurel, and from there to the boundary of a state park. Around them, the subdivisions had grown, but this valley remained. "I have the largest backyard in the world," the man liked to say. The last time he had climbed to the peak was twelve years prior, for his sixtieth birthday, but his physical vigor had long outlasted the functioning of memory, and he could still walk in the valley with his wife, or with Seini. It was thirteen miles to the top, he often told her, just as he told her that the Miwoks of the area had once thought the peak was the center of creation, and that because of the flatness of the surrounding landscape you could watch over everything, could see all the way to the Sierra Nevada, a view farther than from any other mountain in the world.

Later, the old man's wife must have felt it necessary to confirm this. Or at least to confirm that the old man wasn't the only person to say this about the view. It wasn't the height of the mountain, she told Seini, it was its loneliness. This was a funny description, Seini thought, and sensed that it was unintended, and that the old woman was embarrassed she had noticed. So she said nothing, and the old woman continued. She'd been there many times, she said. With her husband. Where they could see clear across the Central Valley, to the thin, white strip of distant mountains, like a tear between earth and sky.

The arrangements of the household had come together quickly, in the second week of the order to shelter in place. Seini had never met the old man's son or grandson prior to their arrival that Tuesday in late March. They lived in San Francisco and visited only rarely, and before the old man's memory of his family closed over completely, he'd told Seini that his son was just too busy, "like his pops." The son had been a great athlete in his youth, the old man said, a baseball player—Seini should have seen him pitch. The old woman had laughed at this and told Seini that the son had been rather mediocre, but that he loved his father more than anything, and the reason he came so infrequently was that it was too painful to see the old man in his dementia. She said this without any bitterness, and Seini understood that she was also speaking for herself.

Given what she knew of the son, Seini had been surprised to hear from the old woman that he would be coming to live with them. But the son, she also learned, had been in the process of getting a divorce when the epidemic struck, and after a week, the couple had found the prospect of further close confinement unbearable. So the son had returned to live with his parents, and brought with him the little boy, who had difficulties with attention and impulsivity, and who, all parties agreed, couldn't last in the San Francisco apartment without his friends, his school, the parks. Seini was aware, listening to the old woman explain this, that there was even more that was not being shared about the son and the boy, and the mother who would assent to giving up her child. But she didn't ask. She'd long ago discovered that she could learn much more about her patients and their families by quietly waiting and watching the outlines fill in.

So there were five of them in the house at the end of the valley of oak and laurel. Before the outbreak, Seini drove home weekly to stay with her husband and their youngest daughter in their home in Redwood City. She had two older girls, too—one who was a nurse and one who worked at a supermarket—and a boy, her little boy, who now was twenty-eight and stood six foot five and was a security guard at San Francisco General. When the outbreak began to spread, the old woman took Seini aside and asked about her home situation, whether it was possible to control whom she came in contact with. Seini thought of her youngest daughter's friends, and her other children's jobs. It was not possible, Seini said, and so she came to live with the old man and woman, and in the evenings FaceTimed with her family, and when this wasn't enough to fill the growing emptiness inside her, once a week, she got in her car and drove the wooded streets, the rolling grasslands, the double-barreled tunnel, the snaking highways, the long, bay-skimming bridge—an hour for a trip that usually took two—and she would park first outside her sister's apartment, and then her own, and talk. On the block where they lived, the buildings were close together, packs of teenage girls roamed in defiance of the isolation orders, and her sister jokingly asked her how it was "out in the woods." But Seini was hardly the only one among their friends who had come to live apart from their family because the people they cared for were frail and they didn't want to bring the disease into those homes.

Prior to the son's arrival, Seini had slept upstairs in the room next to the old man, who because of his nighttime wandering and confusion no longer shared a bed with his wife. It was a big room, with a view of a great backyard fig tree planted when the old man and woman first moved there, and then to the mountain beyond. Long ago, it had been the son's room, and for a moment Seini worried the son would take it back. But he chose a smaller guest room near the kitchen, where he spent his days in front of a laptop. It was clear from the start that whatever animosities had fueled his divorce were far from cooling, and when the son wasn't working, he walked up and down the street outside, arguing into his phone. It was better that he kept his distance from his father, thought Seini. For while the old man no longer recognized these new arrivals, he understood intuitively that there was unhappiness about them, and this confused and frightened him. When the son joined them for dinner, he couldn't resist correcting his father, or looking off when the old man got food on his face, or when he talked endlessly about cardiology and told them the same stories, over and over, about how much the field had changed since he was a medical student. To avoid scaring the old man or the child, they didn't talk about the epidemic, and so the old man repeated his difficult-to-follow stories, and all the others were lost in thought. All the others, that is, except the little boy, who was transfixed.

Seini's realization that the boy did not see his grandfather as she did came surprisingly slowly for someone who prided herself on her implicit understanding of families. She would have thought that anyone would eventually tire of hearing, for the eighth time, how the first EKG, devised by Einthoven, was the size of a small car and required the patient to sit with three limbs in buckets of water, or how the old man had been an intern at Stanford when Shumway performed the first heart transplant in the United States, or how, before the development of echocardiograms, he could estimate the ejection fraction of the left ventricle just by placing his palm on a patient's chest. But the boy—who in most contexts couldn't sit still for three seconds without reaching out and grabbing something, or making a joke, or rocking back and forth in his chair until it almost tipped over, who always talked too loud, too fast, who interrupted or abruptly left the table—the boy was captivated by the stories, loved the repetitions, just like her own son had asked his father to repeat the same tales from his childhood in Tonga. Sometimes, between the old man's stories, the boy would tell one of his own, usually a recounting of the plot of a science fiction series he was reading on his Kindle, full of obscure characters and magic portals, a litany of names and technologies not unlike—Seini decided—the history of cardiology. And the old man would listen and, though he asked no questions, exclaim, "That's right!" and "How about that!"

And so it was that their meals had quickly become a dialogue between two people, and the three in the house who could safely operate a stove or a blender, who read the papers, who had grown increasingly aware of the fragility of life, were quiet and listened and ate.

On FaceTime, at night, when the old man was asleep and the old woman deep in a novel, and before descending the stairs one last time to clean up, Seini would tell her sister about the conversations between the child and the old man. Usually, she didn't talk so much about the families she cared for, but she worried for the boy. Now, on the news, they were saying that school would be closed for the remainder of the spring, and might not open even in the autumn, and she wondered how a child could grow up alone. On the walnut-lined street, there were families with children, and when she and the old man went walking, she watched them playing in their yards. Some evenings, the boy's father took him out to play catch, but the boy had poor coordination, and missed almost every ball, and as he scrambled to fetch them in the hedges, the patches of wild daffodils, the gopher holes, his father snuck glances at his phone. All the boy's classes were over Zoom, and when he was called upon to share something about his life, he spoke enthusiastically and chaotically about the history of cardiology, while his teacher, a woman of Seini's age, sat on a couch and listened with puzzled amusement, her cats slinking menacingly behind her. But usually, the boy just played with the controls of the computer, making Zoom backgrounds with graphics of spaceships he downloaded from the Internet. Or he curled over the Kindle in his lap, lost in his intergalactic world. Other times, his grandmother sat with him and tried to read to him or talk to him, but the moment he was cornered, he climbed onto the top of the couch and tumbled off, or spun in circles, or suddenly decided he wanted ice from the ice maker, filling a glass so violently that the cubes went skidding across the floor.

It was Seini's idea to take the boy on her walks with the old man, and then, because her middle daughter had begun to call her crying each afternoon, to let them go on alone. Her daughter had been a dialysis nurse, but when the outbreak started, she was reassigned to the emergency room. Now, every day, she told her mother she couldn't take it, couldn't take the death, couldn't take the families threatening her when they weren't allowed into the hospital, couldn't take the feeling that her clothes, her hair, her skin, were covered with a poison that would infect her husband and her children. The street was long and mostly empty, and Seini listened as she watched the boy and man ahead of her. She didn't have an answer. But she knew her daughter knew this, knew that if she wanted an answer she would have called her father. "It's fucking unreal," her daughter said, over and over. Seini didn't like cussing and, after several days of tolerance, reminded her. "It's unreal," her daughter said.

In the street, they sometimes passed dog walkers in masks, but there were few cars and the shoulder was wide. At first, Seini felt guilty for hanging back and letting the two of them walk on together, though she didn't know if she was entrusting the child to the old man or the old man to the child. What was clear was that both were happiest in one another's presence, away from the scolding son and the fretting old woman. They made a funny pair. The old man was stocky and broad chested, had thick, gray eyebrows, and wore pressed dress shirts Seini chose for him each morning, an old trick she'd learned to make her patients feel like they were preparing for an occasion, just as she daily shaved their faces and trimmed their hair. The little boy, gangly and mop haired, had come with seven T-shirts, all of which bore the image of either Harry Potter or a character from Star Wars. Even after a month had passed, she couldn't say whether the old man knew that the leaping, loud, endlessly inquisitive child was his grandson, or whether the boy knew that the old man had no memory of what they'd discussed the day before.

The old man, despite his difficulties bathing or dressing, was steady with a pair of hiking poles, and though Seini worried that the child, who skipped and ran circles around him as they walked, would leap onto his grandfather or knock him over, this never happened. What did happen, one day, was that the boy dashed into the street to examine the body of a flattened squirrel, and was nearly hit by a passing car. Seini told no one, but from then on, they took the little path out of the backyard that led down into the valley. She felt less comfortable there: she saw the scat of wild animals, and turkey vultures wobbling in the sky above. But the ease of the old man reassured her. There, she understood, he could rely on instinct, habit, and she reminded herself that he'd known the mountain longer than she'd been alive. Other times, however, she thought of another story he'd told her, this one from his childhood, about a great black wolf that dragged a boy out of his schoolhouse in Circassia while the other children watched. Later, his wife had come and found her in the kitchen to tell her that he'd invented this one, too. The old man was born in Queens, New York; she'd always guessed the story came from his father, who'd passed through Central Asia after his internment in a gulag during the Second World War. A gulag, she added, was a labor camp.

"And did the boy survive?" Seini had asked her.

"The boy?"

"The boy in the story."

"Oh," said the old woman. She paused for a moment and looked at Seini in a way that she hadn't before. "You know, I never asked. But I'm not even sure there was a boy. His father also made things up."

May passed. The leaves grew thick on the walnuts, and green figs budded on the backyard tree. The valley bloomed with California poppy, then white flowers that reminded Seini of the morning glories she would pick in Tonga, and then, in thick patches, a small, blue-violet blossom whose name she didn't know. The days turned warmer, and her asthma flared, and she found herself needing to stop and rest on a long, recumbent branch of laurel, behind a bench that had been wrapped with yellow warning tape. There, the signal was good, and she could listen to her daughter while the old man and the little boy continued along the trail, ten, fifteen minutes to the gate at the end of the valley and back. Soon, she unrolled a little blanket, took off her shoes, and massaged her feet. Fierce, bristling caterpillars stalked among the waving grass, little black-caped birds warily inspected her, and a pair of mushrooms broke the hard clay earth, grew tall, and shriveled in the heat. In the distance, she could hear the boy shouting, or singing, but there was no one nearby to admonish him. If she didn't worry about the old man or his wife, or the little boy, or her son, or her husband or her daughters, she realized she was almost happy.

When the man and boy would return, she'd find them talking about exactly the same things as when they'd left. Sometimes, they were so lost in conversation, or in parallel worlds that didn't involve one another, that they didn't even seem to notice her waiting, and she had to hurry to catch them. Back at the house, the old man would nap and the boy would disappear into his Kindle. And after dinner, they would go out again, each day like the last, the time dissolving, Einthoven, Shumway, and magic portals, until the June evening when Seini lay down beneath the laurel, amid the garrulous company of the birds, and somehow, thoughts slowing in the dry and golden heat, drifted off to sleep.

She was awakened by the scuttling of a squirrel and a cool breeze rising through the valley. At first, she didn't know where she was, and took a moment to register the laurel and the dimming sky. It wasn't the first time she'd fallen asleep there, but it was the deepest she'd slept in a long while, deep enough to dream that she was back in Tonga, only now with the old man and the little boy. They were in the ocean, bobbing up and down, and she was watching from the shore. There was nothing unusual in this; almost all her dreams were about caring for others, seeing them in danger, and trying—with legs that wouldn't move, a voice that couldn't cry for help—to save them. In this one, there was something beautiful about the way they floated in the swells, but the moment that she tried to reach them was the moment she awoke.

She sat up. Dusk was falling. The birds had vanished. Her eyes followed the trail to the final turn before it disappeared behind the oaks, but it was empty. Slipping on her shoes, she stood and gathered the blanket. They must have passed her, as they often did, she thought, and with this thought she felt suddenly faint, and wondered if she had stood too quickly. There was no reason to worry, she told herself, but then her chest was very tight. Instinctively, she rummaged through her purse for her inhaler, until she recalled that with the pandemic her pharmacy had been unable to refill her prescription.

It was only ten minutes back to the house, but with her shortening breath she had to stop twice, and she reached the yard in darkness. Almost instantly, she knew they weren't home yet. Inside, the house was too quiet, and the old man's hiking poles weren't resting against the stairs, where he usually left them. The boy's father was at his laptop, and the old woman was upstairs, talking to one of two different book clubs that gathered over the computer on certain evenings, though when Seini listened, she heard the old woman talking only about her husband. Seini thought of interrupting, of asking for help, and yet she knew that would mean admitting more than just a momentary lapse, it would mean renouncing a central premise that had sustained her, that the world was something that could be tended. She returned outside, and went around to the front of the house. But the street was also empty, empty of the masked dog walkers; even the neighbors' homes seemed abandoned. In her pocket, her phone buzzed, and she fumbled for it, as if the person calling might have an answer for her predicament. But when she looked, she realized she had only imagined it. There was just the time, and the lock-screen photo of her middle daughter sticking out her tongue, a prank she'd played long ago when Seini was still learning to use the iPhone, but an image that, for so much carelessness and joy, she kept.

Still holding her phone, she circled back to the yard, and then beyond to the path, as the view of the peak opened before her. She was walking faster now, down into the valley, where she paused once more. Possibilities rose about her. Wolves pawed the fresh snow; bodies broke through the wave curl; between earth and sky, a magic portal opened. The world turned slowly around the axis of the mountain. Far away, her daughter was laughing again. A wind came over the hills, the trees, the valleys. Her lungs returned and she began to run.

ON SAYING GOODBYE TO POSSIBLY MY FAVORITE PLACE ON EARTH: ON TRATTORIA CONTADINA, AND WHAT A RESTAURANT CAN MEAN

ANTHONY MARRA

2018 JOYCE CAROL OATES PRIZE RECIPIENT

When I moved to California for the second time, I spent several weeks with my aunt Margie—technically, my mom's first cousin—who lived in the East Bay neighborhood of Pleasant Hill. While making lunch one day, I found a rusty butcher's knife in Margie's knife drawer. It was over a foot long and looked like it belonged to a horror movie clown.

"Oh, that'll be Bill's," Margie said, smiling. Bill, Margie's husband, had worked as a teamster delivering papers for the *Oakland Tribune*. Early one morning in the mid-eighties, Bill was dropping off papers down by Lake Merritt when a man tried to kill him. It was winter. He was wearing leather gloves. He grabbed the knife and twisted it from the other man's grip. The other man ran away and Bill stood there holding the butcher's knife by the blade while geese beat their wings around him. He kept it as a trophy and lucky charm. Margie, who tolerates no clutter, told him that knives go in the knife drawer.

Bill was a big guy, always halfway into a story, a dapper dresser who could describe a pair of Ferragamo lace-ups the way a sommelier describes a Brunello. He seemed larger than life, and, in the end, was: he passed of lung cancer a year before I found the knife in the drawer. On the knife's handle Margie has written precisely where and when Bill evaded death. The how and the why she won't forget.

～

Margie's daughter and son-in-law, Gina and Kevin Correnti, own and operate Trattoria Contadina, a North Beach institution that's been in Kevin's family for three generations. It's at the corner of Mason and Union, only a block off Washington Square yet remote enough that any tourist you pass is likely lost. Per square foot, Trattoria Contadina is my favorite place in San Francisco, and, quite possibly, on Earth. It's a place where wedding proposals are regularly popped and graduations celebrated, and simply walking in the door raises your odds of photobombing a fond memory. It's an island of consistency in a changing city. Most days, Gina knows most diners. The "new guy" in the kitchen started in 1986.

Signed photographs of local luminaries, minor celebrities, and regular customers fill the walls. A few weeks ago, Kevin pointed to a faded Little League photograph inscribed to Kevin's father in a child's unsteady handwriting. "That's him now," Kevin said, nodding to the slugger at the bar. "He was signed to the Cardinals last year."

Their bestselling dish at present is Il Diavolo, a penne pasta with 'nduja, burrata, shredded basil, and a spicy tomato sauce. The recipe came to Kevin one night in a dream—this is also how the melody of "Yesterday" came to Paul McCartney, and both masterpieces carry me to similar heights of nostalgia (as my floridness attests). It makes me remember great-aunt Giuseppina's kitchen, or the stories my father tells from his childhood; it is a day pass to a world I descend from but do not belong to.

When you're halfway finished, Gina comes by to ask how your meal is. The question is less a matter of culinary enjoyment than one of mental competence, like knowing the correct year and sitting president. It is a question to which there is but one answer: "It's perfect."

There is one frame without a picture. It's not on the restaurant's walls, but directly across the street, in Gina and Kevin's apartment. One day, while moving furniture, they found jotted measurements Bill had penciled on the wall when he helped Gina move in nearly twenty years ago. Gina bought a tiny frame, and set it over her father's handwriting. If asked, she might say her father had been an artist.

~

I'd hoped to live in North Beach, but unless you're grandfathered into the neighborhood through rent control, it's largely unaffordable to the literary community that, along with Italians, made the neighborhood famous.

Instead, I moved to lovely, leafy north Oakland, into an old Craftsman divided into four units. It's a perfect area for walking: to the coffee shop, or the bookstore, or the bar where on a Monday five years ago I met the love of my life, a Californian who is bringing me back east next fall.

As we discuss what we will bring and what we will leave, the biggest question has been the books. There are so many: beneath the bed, in the closet, lining the crawl space, towering on shelves, steadying the coffee table. They weigh many times more than the two of us combined.

One of those Little Free Libraries has recently appeared at the end of my block. It looks like a birdhouse for books. Now, on my walks, I leave a book or two inside. My large personal library evaporates, book by book, into this little public one. When the time comes, I'll be light enough to leave.

The problem is that the little library seems to manufacture more marvelous books, and despite my intentions, I can't resist the dog-eared Hilary Mantel, or the Toni Morrison annotated by a diligent student, or the Swedish thriller bookmarked with a takeout menu. I imagine that my own library is reassembled, book by book, inside a stranger's home, and theirs is reassembled in mine, like tapestries we trade thread-by-thread through a keyhole. Every day, as I prepare to leave, I find another reason to stay.

Many of the Italians who built North Beach were "birds of passage," young men who came to America intending to work awhile and then return to Italy. Many were illiterate and dictated their correspondence to professional letter writers. Back in the old country, other letter writers—or the village priest—would read the letters to their recipients and transcribe their replies. Some birds of passage returned home, while others stayed in North Beach and started restaurants. Over a long correspondence, the letter writers on either end would come to identify their counterpart through penmanship, grammatical errors, favored words. Perhaps they would wait as anxiously as the recipient for the next chapter to arrive. Over a long correspondence, two distant letter writers might live as neighbors on either side of a story, speaking only through the words of strangers that passed through their hands.

I am not leaving until the end of the year, but already I know how I will spend my last hours as a citizen of California. I will have dinner at Trattoria Contadina and then, in the morning, I'll head to the airport. But on my way, I will leave this very volume in the Little Free Library at the end of my block. It will be the last book I leave behind, and I hope you read these words, neighbor, because we have exchanged so much but never our names, and it is beautiful to at last meet you, in this sentence, while there is time to say goodbye.

CONTRIBUTORS

Michelle Alas (she/her) is a second-year at Brown University who grew up in the San Francisco Bay Area, where she took part in a Simpson Workshop. She is lover of reading, writing, and running. As a Salvadoran-American, Michelle enjoys writing about her culture and her family. Michelle is a strong advocate for educational equity and social justice.

Alison (Kimi) Andre is a senior at Northgate High School. She is a leader in the drama program and organizer of slam poetry events at Northgate and elsewhere.

Lauren Bausley will be entering her junior year at Northgate High School, where she is active in drama and sports.

Lorne M. Buchman is president of ArtCenter College of Design in Pasadena, California, and an international leader in art and design education. He is also a theater director, dramatic literature professor, and the author of a book on filmic adaptations of Shakespeare's plays. He hosts *Change Lab: Conversations on Transformation and Creativity*, a podcast in which he conducts interviews with leading artists, designers, and cultural innovators. Buchman previously served on the faculty of University of California, Berkeley, and as president of both Saybrook University and California College of the Arts. He holds a PhD from Stanford University in Drama and Humanities.

Liam Casey, a graduate of Northgate High School, is a freshman at the University of Southern California, majoring in Cinematic Arts. He enjoys hiking, spending time with friends, listening to music and watching classic films. He hopes to pursue a career within the film industry as either a producer or a director.

Diane Del Signore is the inaugural executive director of New Literary Project. She has had extensive experience leading both nonprofit and corporate teams. She directed for over ten years global partnerships for Hewlett-Packard, managing a worldwide team of sales, marketing, and technical personnel. Then for ten years she served as executive director of a statewide nonprofit dedicated to sustainable agriculture. Over her entire professional career, she has been actively involved with nonprofit boards devoted to arts, education, and community health. Beyond that, Diane is an urban farmer, raising goats, chickens, rabbits; she also teaches cooking classes with her local 4-H club. She is a Stanford University MBA, and throughout her life she has cultivated love and admiration of writers and writing, teachers and teaching. diane@simpsonliteraryproject.org

Amanda Dimicola took part in a Simpson Workshop at Northgate High School.

Joseph Di Prisco is Founder and Chair of New Literary Project and Series Editor of *Simpsonistas*. He is the author of fiction, prize-winning poetry, memoir, and nonfiction. His most recent works include *Sightlines from the Cheap Seats* (poems), *The Pope of Brooklyn* (memoir), and *The Good Family Fitzgerald* (a novel). He grew up in Brooklyn and then in Berkeley, where he received his PhD from UC Berkeley. He has taught English and creative writing, from middle school and high school and through college and beyond, and has served as Trustee or Chair of nonprofit boards devoted to education, the arts, theater, and children's mental health. jdp@newliteraryproject.org

Danielle Evans was the 2021 Joyce Carol Oates Prize Recipient. She is the author of the story collections *The Office of Historical Corrections* and *Before You Suffocate Your Own Fool Self*. Her first collection won the PEN American Robert W. Bingham Prize, the Hurston-Wright award for fiction, and the Paterson Prize for fiction; her second won the Janet Heidinger Kafka Prize and The Bridge Book Award and was a finalist for The Aspen Prize, The Story Prize, and The LA Times Book prize for fiction. She was a 2020 National Endowment for the Arts fellow, and a 2011 National Book Foundation 5 under 35 honoree. Her stories have appeared in magazines including *The Paris Review, A Public Space,*

American Short Fiction, Callaloo, The Sewanee Review, and *Phoebe,* and have been anthologized in *The Best American Short Stories* 2008, 2010, 2017, and 2018, and in *New Stories From The South.* She received an MFA in fiction from the Iowa Writers Workshop, previously taught creative writing at American University in Washington DC and the University of Wisconsin, Madison, and currently teaches in The Writing Seminars at Johns Hopkins University.

Charlotte Feehan is currently a junior at Northgate High School

Lise Gaston is a former Simpson Fellow, and the author of the poetry collection *Cityscapes in Mating Season* (Signature Editions). Her work has appeared in journals across America, Canada, and Ireland, and has been awarded the Harold Taylor Prize from the League of American Poets and the 2021 CBC Poetry Prize. She received her PhD from UC Berkeley in 2019. Lise currently lives in Vancouver, Canada.

Lauren Groff is the 2022 Joyce Carol Oates Prize Recipient. She is the author of six books of fiction, the most recent the novel *Matrix* (September 2021). Her work has won The Story Prize, the ABA Indies' Choice Award, and France's Grand Prix de l'Héroïne, was a three time finalist for the National Book Award for Fiction and twice for the Kirkus Prize, and was shortlisted for the National Book Critics Circle Prize, the Southern Book Prize, and the Los Angeles Times Prize. She has received fellowships from the Guggenheim Foundation and the Radcliffe Institute for Advanced Study, and was named one of Granta's Best of Young American Novelists. Her work has been translated into over thirty languages. She lives in Gainesville, Florida.

Sofia Kohn is a 2022 graduate of Northgate High School and will be pursuing her writing as a student at University of Denver in the fall.

Ryan Lackey, a Simpson Fellow, is a PhD student in English at the University of California, Berkeley. His writing has appeared in *Public Books, Kenyon Review, Commonweal,* the *Los Angeles Review of Books, Cream City Review,* and elsewhere.

Jessica Laser was born in Chicago. She is the author of two books of poems: *Planet Drill* (forthcoming, Futurepoem Books), winner of the Other Futures Award, and *Sergei Kuzmich from All Sides* (2019, Letter Machine Editions). Recent work has appeared in *The Yale Review, Lana Turner, The Cortland Review, The Volta, Blazing Stadium, Rainbow Agate* and *Solar.* A graduate of the Iowa Writers' Workshop, she is currently a PhD candidate in English at the University of California, Berkeley, where she was a Spring 2022 Simpson Fellow with the New Literary Project.

Bethany Leong: "I am a Northgate student going into my junior year. I love to draw and animate with a dream of working in the animation industry. I have grown to love writing also. My likes and dislikes shift around like the flow of words in a piece of writing. It's about giving it a chance or two."

Ralph J. Long Jr. is the author of two chapbooks, *Polaroids at a Yard Sale* (Main Street Rag Press, 2021) and *A Democracy Divided* (Poetry Box, 2018). His work has appeared in the anthology *Ambrosia: A Conversation About Food* and *Common Ground Review, Humble Pie, Stoneboat Literary Journal, Scriblerus, Sisyphus, Ursa Minor* and *Zingara Poetry Review* and elsewhere. Born in Brooklyn, New York, a graduate of Haverford College, he lives in Oakland with his wife, Liz.

Olivia Loscavio is a twenty-year-old Bay Area native, and a junior at Occidental College. *Simpsonistas Vol. 4* marks her fourth year happily spent with the New Literary Project. When she is not writing lesbian poetry she can be found reading, tending to her plants, and spending time with her partner.

Ian S. Maloney is Director of the Jack Hazard Fellowships. He is Professor of Literature, Writing, and Publishing at St. Francis College in Brooklyn, NY; writes reviews for *Vol. 1 Brooklyn*; and serves on the Literary Council for the Brooklyn Book Festival and as Community Outreach Director for the Walt Whitman Initiative. He recently completed his first novel, *South Brooklyn Exterminating.* ian@newliteraryproject.org

Akira Marks is seventeen years old at the time of writing and has always been passionate about the arts. Till his freshman year of high school,

Akira had been aiming for a career in animation. However, his visual arts skills manifested into filmmaking instead. In the summer of 2022, he had the opportunity to have a deeper education with filmmaking by making a short film with BAVC Media in San Francisco. Now, with the experience of publishing a short story, Akira is ready to hone his writing and drama skills to greater heights—and hopefully finish one of his work-in-progress screenplays.

Anthony Marra was the 2018 Joyce Carol Oates Prize Recipient. He is the New York Times bestselling author of *The Tsar of Love and Techno* and *A Constellation of Vital Phenomena*, winner of the National Book Critics Circle's John Leonard Prize and the Anisfield-Wolf Book Award, and longlisted for the National Book Award. His new novel, *Mercury Pictures Presents*, was published in August 2022.

Daniel Mason was the 2020 Joyce Carol Oates Prize Recipient. He is a physician and author of *The Piano Tuner* (2002), *A Far Country* (2007), *The Winter Soldier* (2018), and *A Registry of My Passage Upon the Earth* (2020), which was a finalist for the Pulitzer Prize. His work has been translated into twenty-eight languages, awarded a 2021 Guggenheim Fellowship, the California Book Award, the Northern California Book Award, and a Fellowship from the National Endowment for the Arts. *The Piano Tuner* was produced as an opera by Music Theatre Wales for the Royal Opera House in London, and adapted to the stage by Lifeline Theatre in Chicago. His short stories and essays have appeared in *The Atlantic, Harper's, Zoetrope: All Story, Zyzzyva, Narrative*, and *Lapham's Quarterly*, and have been awarded a Pushcart Prize, a National Magazine Award and an O. Henry Prize. An assistant professor in the Stanford University Department of Psychiatry, his research and teaching interests include the subjective experience of mental illness and the influence of literature, history, and culture on the practice of medicine.

Katharine Ogden Michaels is the lead author of *Strong Ties: Barclay Simpson and the Pursuit of the Common Good in Business and Philanthropy*, written with Judith Adamson, published in 2022 by Rare Bird Books. A study in ethical leadership, *Strong Ties* focuses on the set of convictions that allowed Oakland native, Barclay Simpson, to build a successful, international, publicly-traded company from nothing and to become one of the leading philanthropists in the San Francisco Bay Area. Katharine is the lead writer of *The Gambler*, a 1997 dramatic film written in collaboration with famed Director Károly Makk, that won awards at the Brussels, Emden, and Festroia-Troia International Film Festivals. From 2012 to the present, she has regularly published essays in the literary quarterly *The Threepenny Review*, and has recently written an introduction to a new Italian translation of the Joseph Conrad novel *The Mirror of the Sea*, published by Rizzoli in June 2021. She is the coauthor of *Rembrandt*, a Catalogue for a 1989 show of original prints by the artist at the Barclay Simpson Art Gallery in Lafayette, CA. Literary Executor and Editor for the work of award-winning writer Leonard Michaels, she published with Farrar, Straus, and Giroux, selected fiction and non-fiction collections of Leonard Michaels' work in 2007 and 2009. Since 1990 she has restored antique stone farmhouses and villas in Umbria and Tuscany, Italy, and continues to manage several of these properties for the partnerships that own them, splitting her time between Berkeley, CA and Umbria, Italy. She received a BA *magna cum laude* from Yale University, a member of the first group of women to be admitted to Yale College, and received her Master's degree in English and American Literature from UC Berkeley.

Mia Allyson Montifar is beginning her junior year at Northgate High School

Anna Moraru graduated from Northgate High School in 2022. She plans to attend DVC in the Fall. An immigrant from Ukraine, she has written extensively for the *Northgate Sentinel* about the Ukrainian War.

John Murray was born and raised in New England and now lives in Los Angeles. As a professor in the undergraduate writing program at the University of Southern California, he taught academic writing with an emphasis on community collaboration and social justice issues for over two decades. Murray also cofounded creative writing workshops for recently paroled prisoners who were serving life sentences. His essays and short stories have appeared in several publications, and he is currently working on a collection of short stories. He's pleased to serve on the New Literary Project Board.

Gabrielle Nicolas is a graduated senior from Northgate High School now heading into freshman year at UC Berkeley. Any form of creative expression has always been incredibly important to her whether it is theatre, painting, singing, dancing, or creative writing. It's an outlet for emotions and experiences, and a way to connect with others. In her last year of high school, she lost her father unexpectedly at the beginning of the school year. Nothing Gabrielle said could describe everything she was going through. So she tried writing it instead. The piece she wrote is in dedication to her loving dad and her journey through this past year. "No matter what happens, I will always be here." -Eric Nicolas.

Joyce Carol Oates is Joyce Carol Oates. She is an Honorary member of the Board of Directors of New Literary Project, a recipient of the National Humanities Medal, the National Book Critics Circle Ivan Sandrof Lifetime Achievement Award, the National Book Award, and the 2019 Jerusalem Prize for Lifetime Achievement, and has been nominated several times for the Pulitzer Prize. She has written some of the most enduring fiction of our time, including the national best sellers *We Were the Mulvaneys; Blonde;* and the *New York Times* best seller *The Falls,* which won the 2005 Prix Femina. In 2020 she was awarded the Cino Del Duca World Prize for Literature. She is the Roger S. Berlind '52 Distinguished Professor of the Humanities emerita at Princeton University and has been a member of the American Academy of Arts and Letters since 1978.

Mikaela Pasalo took part in the Simpson Workshop at Cal Prep.

Cristal Reyes-Moran took part in the Simpson Workshop at Cal Prep.

Lily Sanchez will be entering her senior year at Northgate High School. She is active in journalism and writes essays for fun!!!

A. R. Taylor is an award-winning playwright, essayist, and fiction writer. Her debut novel, *Sex, Rain, and Cold Fusion,* won a Gold Medal for Best Regional Fiction at the Independent Publisher Book Awards 2015 and was a USA Best Book Awards finalist. In addition, it was named one of the twelve Most Cinematic Books of 2014 by *Kirkus Reviews*. Her second novel, *Jenna Takes the Fall*, was published by She Writes Press in 2020 and received the 2021 Readers' Favorite Bronze Medal in the Fiction–Intrigue genre. She's been published in the *Los Angeles Times, the Southwest Review, Pedantic Monthly, The Cynic* online magazine, the *Berkeley Insider, So It Goes*—the Kurt Vonnegut Memorial Library Magazine on Humor, *Red Rock Review*, and *Rosebud*. In her past life, Taylor was head writer on two Emmy-winning series for public television. She has performed at the Gotham Comedy Club in New York, Tongue & Groove in Hollywood, and Lit Crawl LA. You can find her video blog, *Trailing Edge: Ideas Whose Time Has Come and Gone* at her website www.lonecamel.com. Her latest novel, *Call Me When You're Dead*, appeared in September 2022.

Viviana Varela took part in the Simpson Workshop at Girls Inc. of Alameda County.

Noah Warren, a Simpson Fellow, was born in Nova Scotia, Canada. He is the author of *The Complete Stories*, published by Copper Canyon in 2021, and *The Destroyer in the Glass*, chosen by Carl Phillips for the 2016 Yale Series of Younger Poets. His work has been supported by fellowships from Yale, Stanford, The New Literary Project, and the Arts Research Center. He is a PhD candidate in English at UC Berkeley, where he coordinates the Lunch Poems Reading Series.

His poems appear in *The Paris Review, POETRY, The American Poetry Review, Ploughshares, ZYZZYVA, PEN America, The New England Review, The Southern Review, AGNI, poets.org*, and elsewhere. At Berkeley, his research explores the occasions of poetry in the American nineteenth century. He is at work on a novel and a new collection of poems.

Kaitlin Weitl is a Northgate High School student with a passion for writing poetry. When she is not writing, she can be found swimming, reading mystery books, and attending various Broadway musicals with her family. Kaitlin is also a coffee aficionado and loves to explore new coffee shops all across California, her home state.

David Wood has taught English at Northgate High School since 1984, and is a member of the New Literary Project Board; he also served on the jury for the Joyce Carol Oates Prize. He was a board member and board president of the celebrated Aurora Theatre Company, and now serves on the Advisory Board for the Kalmanovitz School of Education at Saint Mary's College of California. A Yale graduate and University of Chicago M.A., he estimates he is coming up on his hundredth year of teaching. "So it goes."

Michelle Zyarko is a senior at Northgate High School.

NEW
LITERARY
PROJECT

Drive social change, unleash artistic power, lift up a literate, democratic society. Please support NewLit.

Visit our website: https://www.newliteraryproject.org/donate

Or mail your donation:
New Literary Project
4100 Redwood Road, Suite 20A/424
Oakland, CA 94619
EIN: 84-3898853

Diane Del Signore, Executive Director
diane@newliteraryproject.org

Thank you. Your generosity makes all the difference.

Write and read your heart out.